A Million Premonitions

poems by
Viktor Sosnora

translated from the Russian by
DINARA GEORGEOLIANI
& MARK HALPERIN

ZEPHYR PRESS
Brookline, MA

Cover art by Bobbie Halperin
Book design by *typeslowly*
Printed by Cushing Malloy

Several of these poems appeared previously in the following journals:
*Agni, American Poetry Review, Chicago Review, Denver Quarterly,
International Poetry Review,* and in the Zephyr anthology *In the Grip of
Strange Thoughts: Russian Poetry in a New Era.*

Zephyr Press acknowledges with gratitude the financial support
of Charles Merrill, the Massachusetts Cultural Council, and the
National Endowment for the Arts.

NATIONAL
ENDOWMENT
FOR THE ARTS   massculturalcouncil.org

Library of Congress Control Number: 2004100898

08 07 06 05 04   98765432 FIRST EDITION

ZEPHYR PRESS
50 Kenwood Street
Brookline, MA 02446
www.zephyrpress.org

Table of Contents

During a writing career of more than forty years, Viktor Aleksandrovich Sosnora has remained faithful to himself — his poetry doesn't resemble that of anyone else in Russian literature. Although he is a contemporary of Alexander Kushner and Joseph Brodsky — members of the circle of Akhmatova, who have carried forward the Acmeist agenda of formal and semantic clarity — Sosnora continues a different, experimental side of the Petersburg poetic tradition.

Viktor Sosnora was born in 1936 in Alupka, in the Crimea, owing, he has said, to his mother's belief that Leningrad was no place for a child. The family returned, however, shortly after that. During the Leningrad Blockade, Sosnora's father, a professional acrobat and aerialist, was a commander of ski troops. In 1942 the young Sosnora was sent to his Estonian grandmother and from there to an uncle, the leader of a band of partisans. He witnessed their deaths, and saved himself only by playing dead. After the war, Sosnora joined his father in Warsaw and received his earliest education in Polish. Subsequently, he learned most Slavic languages, Greek, Latin, and a number of West European languages. In Lvov, he attended a sports-school and studied music at the Institute of Applied Arts.

Sosnora returned to Leningrad, served in the army (1955-58), and, while working as a mechanic, studied at the Philosophical Faculty of Leningrad State University. His first poem was published in 1958, during the "Thaw." His first collection, *January Downpour*, appeared in 1962. The critic V. Novikov wrote in *Ogonek* in 1996, "In the mid 60s, when no one had heard of postmodernism, [Sosnora] entered into a daring poetic dialogue with the classics, rewriting both Lermontov and Wilde, and relocating Pushkin's 'Gypsy' in our time." In 1967 Sosnora backed Solzhenitsyn's letter to the IV USSR Writers' Congress. "By that time," reads an article in the *Krugosvet Encyclopedia*, "Sosnora had written many works, which were not published as much from political considerations as their extreme poetic complexity. Finding himself under suspicion by the authorities . . . in a class by himself, 'an esthetic dissident,' he endured his solitude stoically." He published his books in *samizdat*, adorning them with India ink drawings.

Sosnora has translated the poetry of Catullus, Wilde, Poe, Louis Aragon, and Allen Ginsberg into Russian. In 1970 and 1979 he lectured in Paris on Old Russian poetics; and in 1987, in the United States. The 1990s saw much of his work from 1960-1980 first appear in print. He has now published more than a dozen volumes of poetry and prose. His collected poems, *Nine Books* (St. Petersburg, 2002), received the prestigious Apollon Grigoriev Award from the Academy of Russian Contemporary Literature.

Although Sosnora's early poems are romantic and lyrical, with metaphors based on familiar images — trees, bushes, leaves, hills, and domestic backyards — he had already started his journey as an experimentalist. For example, in his poem "Seventeen Years Later," the 11th line reads: "Книги вервьем связал. Не листал. [Knigi verv'em svyazal. Ne listal.] [You bound books with a rope. Didn't page through them.]." Who didn't page through the books, the "I" or the "You"? The poems of this period are frequently written in the first person, which heightens the sense of the personal. Sosnora creates a background of hope, unexpectedly switches to despair, and then withdraws, as in "House Of Hopes." This poem describes a wise house, perhaps the world itself, devoid of slanderers, blockheads, loners, where infamy, power and flattery don't lure. Alas, the speaker doesn't live in this house. He does exist, he insists, but elsewhere.

Sosnora's early poems display a fondness for historical material, Hellas, Rome and medieval Russia—a fondness that continues throughout the body of his work. His experiments with Russian grammar, syntax, and semantics develop a unique style making use of neologisms and metaphors, reflecting his vision of the world. Among the metaphors are "September's" "Море абордажами не обладаю [abordazhami ne obladayu]," indicating lack of protection. We were able to preserve much of the image with "Seas don't provide boardings." The simile from "The Soldiers are Leaving," "Мы в Альпы прошли, как в цветочки [My v Alpy proshli, kak v tsvetochki]" compares entering the Alps to coming into flowers, a garden. The sense is, it's "a piece of cake." That, however, seemed too American for the context and we resorted to the blander "we easily entered the Alps." Earlier, in "Letters from the Forest," the speaker says "I've become so quiet, and not in love, / I play with letters." This refers to the previous stanza, which is in quotes and palindromic. Rather than translating Sosnora's words and losing the self-reflective aspect, we have substituted our own palindromic phrases.

The pace of Sosnora's early poems is unhurried. He takes the reader cautiously through their images. In some of his poems Sosnora intensifies this leisurely pace by repeating while adding: "I lit seven oil lamps, / I lit seven bedside lamps. / I lit seven glassy white lamps / and cleaned my desk." ("Prologue") or "I've seen ten books / on the steppe, / in the saddle. / seen ten necks and ten knives." ("Seventeen Years Later").

Traditional Russian images and Old Russian words appear throughout Sosnora's poems. We have either supplied explanatory notes or used descriptive phrases in the former case. In the case of Old Russian, we have sometimes been fortunate enough to find equivalents. Sosnora's "буквица [bukvitsa]," Old Russian for "letter," we translate as "rune." When, however, he uses Old Russian "отыдь [otyd']" for "to leave someone alone," we simply employ modern English. A more complex use of Old Russian appears in stanza 3, section 4 of "Letters from the Forest." "Зегзица [zegzitsa]" is employed in place of the standard Russian for "cuckoo," and when Sosnora mentions prisons, he "leaps over" the meaning of "cuckoo" to suggest "informant," which is what the *Dictionary of Prison Slang* gives for "cuckoo." The use of Old Russian here implies that the custom is itself old. We "leap" with him and render it "stool-pigeon."

A different mood characterizes Sosnora's later poems. He rarely communicates directly with his reader. His personal "I" often becomes a "we" or is obscure. He tries to find sense in the chaos of the world by creating a new style that employs unexpected images and metaphors, which are at times quite scary. Despair and bitterness keep close company. We have entered a "world frozen in swords," "with no blood in our muscles, only a haze," and its people, "with mouths sewn up," live where there is "an electron and a nuclear megaphone / like a ghost — hang over roofs of the country" and "a virus with an encircling mouth" ("The Soldiers Are Leaving").

As Yakob Gordin justly points out in his introduction to Sosnora's collected poems of 1989, *Return to the Sea*, "The work of V. Sosnora of most recent years turns out to be at the intersection of two traditions — Aseev's play with phonetics, and Khlebnikov's play with semantics." We realized from the very start that keeping Sosnora's sonic devices was one of the most difficult tasks we faced. His sound is more than ornamental. Sometimes he organizes a stanza by repetition of a word-root; at other times, he links phrases through word play. Such tactics are rarely convertible. Still, we have tried to preserve a sense of his techniques. The first line and title of the poem "Eros wouldn't rouse," "Эрос не рос [Eros nye ros]," could be translated, "Eros didn't (or wouldn't) grow." But the sound-play on "ros" would be lost. We've chosen to keep Sosnora's play with "r" and "s" by using "rouse" instead. Similarly, although we have not reproduced Sosnora's rhythms, we have been attentive to them. "In February" approximates the rhyme scheme and metrical structure of the original more closely than is our general practice.

In his more recent poems Sosnora experiments even more heavily with the grammatical norms of Russian. While rhyme and meter recur, the poems typically employ a rhythmical and sonically rich free verse. Some syntactic forms, though irregular in Russian, had no effect on translation since English verbs in the past tense are not sensitive to person or number markings. In the third line, second stanza of "The Soldiers are Leaving," for example, Sosnora writes "И клялся Антоний стоять на нога / и офицеры. [I klyalsya Antonit stoyat' na noga / I ofitsery]," breaking the essential connection between the subject and predicate. While the predicate is in the singular (клялся), the subject is plural (Антоний и офицеры). We didn't keep Sosnora's word order, and chose instead to adhere to standard English structure: "Both Anthony and the officers vowed / to remain firm."

Striking metaphors, very much the poet's own, fill Sosnora's poetry. They articulate his attitude, mood, and perspective. A dictionary can tell us nothing about such words and word combinations; we must understand them in context. When, in the next to the last line of "Seventeen Years Later," Sosnora writes: "забирай меня под забралом [zabiraj menya pod zabralom]," literally "take me under a war helmet's grill (guarding the face)," he is fashioning a metaphor for protection. We tried to produce a similar effect by focusing on "take under" and transforming the rest to read "shelter me under your wing." In "Poet," Sosnora describes a poet "living under an oak," then contrasts that, in the last lines of stanza one, with "But often in this empty-handed life / come luxury, the mountains of Georgia, bottomless money." "Килек клев [kilek klev]" is one of his metaphors here. The unit is based on irony, its components opposed — "sprat," a tiny fish, and "one caught on, or striking a hook." The combination refers to something that does not exist; anyone who attempts to catch a sprat on a hook will be left "empty-handed," our version.

Historical allusions in Sosnora's poetry are often at the crossroads of different cultures. In "Poet," the lines "like a Georgian knight, under a hide I lay / to write in a language of Georgian Queen Tamar" refer to the Georgian epic, "The Knight in the Panther

Skin" by Shota Rustaveli. This information, and other allusions to Russian and Roman history, have been addressed in the notes. But Sosnora can be even more challenging. His reference to Romulus Augustulus as "Agustishka," is, in context, an insulting diminutive. We have supplied the full Latin name, and added a belittling adjective. Even within Russian culture, Sosnora can prove elusive, echoing a literary heritage that an American reader is unlikely to sense. For example, the last line of "Summer Garden by Day, "не гаснет, дивный гений [ne gasnet, divnyj genij] [divine genius, not dying]," plays off Lermontov's elegy for Pushkin, "The Death of the Poet," the line: "Угас… дивный гений [Ugas… divnyj genij] [divine genius has died]."

By dropping subjects, predicates, and/or prepositions, Sosnora often reduces sentences to fragments or even to phrases. We left such structures unchanged since ellipsis may be even more common in English than it is in Russian poetry. In the eleventh line, the second stanza of "Poet," Sosnora writes: "Рукой Харона — водный колорит! — / переводить за руку в рощу пары [Rukoj Kharona —vodnyj kolorit! — / perevodit za ruku v roshchu pary] [Charon conveying couples across to the grove / is such a picturesque water-scene!]" This sentence contains neither a subject nor a predicate. Sosnora's use of instrumental case (Рукой Харона) indicates that an action has been performed by Charon. We worked from there.

We wish to thank our editor, Jim Kates, for offering invaluable suggestions and spurring us on to English versions we would not otherwise have found. We are very grateful to Viktor Aleksandrovich Sosnora himself, for answers to the questions we put to him. It was he who advised us to drop or change references whenever we thought it would better serve an English-speaking reader.

Dinara Georgeoliani
Mark Halperin   *January 2004*

Гусли Бояна

У Бояна
           стозвонные
гусли,
а на гуслях
               русский орнамент,
гусли могут стенать, как гуси,
могут
       и клекотать
орлами,
могут мудростью
с дубом спорить,
спорить скоростью
с волком
           могут,
радость князю – ликуют,
горе –
разом с князем горестно молкнут.
У Бояна
           бойкие струны!
Словно десять кречетов
статных
напускает Боян
               на юное
                       лебединое стадо.

Первый кречет
               кричит победно
песню-здравицу в честь Мстислава,
что прирезал Редедю
пред полками косогов бравых.
То не десять кречетов
юных –

Boyan's *Gusli*

Boyan's *gusli* has
                    resounding
sounds,
on them
a Russian ornament;
the *gusli* can groan like geese,
can
      also screech
like eagles,
can compete
with the oak in wisdom,
can compete
with the wolf
            in speed;
when the prince is gleeful—the *gusli* rejoices,
when he grieves—
it grows sadly silent with his sorrow.
Boyan has
            brisk strings!
It's as if Boyan,
sets
ten stately merlins.
                  on a flock of
                        young swans.
The first merlin
            screams triumphantly
a glorifying song in honor of Mstislav,
who mortally stabbed Prince Rededya
before the regiments of brave Adygei.
Those are not ten
young merlins—

десять пальцев,

                      от песен скорченных,

задевают струны,

                        а струны

сами славу князьям рокочут.

Или вдруг

             заструятся

                            грустью,

журавлиною перекличкою...

У Бояна стозвонные гусли –

пере-

           лив-

                ча-

                    тые!

deformed by playing songs
                          those are ten fingers—
which touch the strings,
                    and the strings themselves
roar glory to the princes.
Or suddenly the strings
                      flow
                          with sorrow,
with cranes calling to each other…
Boyan's *gusli* has resounding sounds—
mo-
    du-
        la-
            ting!

Калика

Посох тук-тук...
Плетется калика,
      посох тук-тук...
в портянках плетенных,
      посох тук-тук,
стихарь да коврига,
      посох тук-тук,
у калики в плетенке.

За плечом
летописные списки
о российских
      ликующих кликах.
Напевая
стишок
      византийский,
вперевалку
плетется калика.

Над каликой
гогочут вприсядку
дядьки-ваньки
и девки-нахалки,
и кусают
      калику за пятки
шелудивые псы-зубоскалы.

      Посох тук-тук
по сухому суглинку,
      посох тук-тук
по кремнистому насту.

Kalika

        The staff click-clacks…
Kalika trudges,
        the staff click-clacks…
in woven foot-wrappings,
        the staff click-clacks,
surplice and loaf—
        the staff click-clacks—
in kalika's bag.

Over his shoulder
are chronicle rolls
of the Russian
        triumphant cliques.
Kalika trudges,
waddling
        as he hums
a Byzantine
jingle.

Doing a squatting dance,
Uncle-Ivans
and insolent wenches
cackle over kalika,
and mangy, snarling dogs
        bite
the minstrel's heels.

        The staff click-clacks
along dry land,
        the staff click-clacks
along the gravelly crust.

Непутево
плетется калика.
Ничего-то
калике не надо.

Kalika trudges
aimlessly.
Kalika needs
nothing.

Обращение

Подари мне еще десять лет,
десять лет,
        да в степи,
                да в седле.

Подари мне еще десять книг,
да перо,
        да кнутом
             да стегни.

Подари мне еще десять шей,
десять шей
да десять ножей.

Срежешь первую шею – живой,
срежешь пятую шею – живой,
лишь умоюсь водой дождевой,
а десятую срежешь –
                мертв.

Не дари оживляющих влаг
или скоропалительных солнц, –
лишь родник,
        да сентябрь,
             да кулак
неизменного солнца.
И все.

Appeal

Grant me ten more years,
ten years
        on the steppe,
                and in the saddle.

Grant me ten more books,
and a pen,
        and whip me
              with a knout.

Grant me ten more necks,
ten necks
and ten knives.

Cut the first neck—I'm alive,
cut the fifth neck—I'm alive,
I need only wash with rainwater,
but cut the tenth—
              I'm dead.

Don't grant me reviving moisture
or hasty suns,—
only spring water,
          September,
             and the fist
of the immutable sun.
That's all.

Семнадцать лет спустя

Десять книг
              да в степи
                              да в седле,
десять шей и ножей отвидал.
«Подари мне еще десять лет»,–
отписал.
Ты семнадцать отдал.

Отнял степь
              да седло
                           да жену.
Книги верьвем связал. Не листал.
Отъял шеи –
                    оставил одну.
Ночью каинств и ламп не лишил.

Что мне делать с ней, шеей, с ножом?
Я не раб,
             я не враг,
                       бой не бью.
Бог с тобой, если Именем – нам:
отдал – отъял и...
Благодарю.

Где ж я был? – В сталактитах у скал?
Чрез семнадцать вернулся. Я – тот.
Те ж народы... Никто не узнал,
для ВЕРХОВНОГО ЧАСА – никто.

Seventeen Years Later

(Appeal)

I've seen ten books
                on the steppe,
                          in the saddle.
seen ten necks and ten knives.
"Grant me ten more years,"—
That's what I wrote.
You gave me seventeen.

You took away the steppe
                the saddle
                        and my wife.
You bound books with a rope. Didn't page through them.
You took away my necks—
                    left only one,
though I could still be a Cainist and use lamps at night.

What can I do with a neck, with a knife?
I'm no slave,
              no enemy,
                        I don't fight fights.
So be it, if you act in His name:
you granted, you took away and…
Thank you.

Where have I been?—In the stalactites by the cliffs?
Seventeen years later, I returned, the same me,
the same people … No one recognized me,
no one at the SUPREME HOUR.

Те дары не расплавлю кольцом.
Не жалей у ножа,
ожидай.
Дай два ока – закроюсь лицом.
Если
      есть
           во мне,–
не оживляй.

Дай два Огня,
           два Зверя,
                    два Дня.
Две волны,
          двойню губ
                да весло.
Не удваивай в Доме меня.
Забирай под забралом,–
и все.

I won't melt those gifts with a ring.
Don't feel sorry at knifepoint,
wait.
Give me two eyes—I'll cover myself with a face.
If
    there's still life
                    in me,—
don't revive it.

Give me two Fires
                    two Beasts,
                                    two Days.
Two waves,
                two sets of lips
                        and an oar.
Don't clone me in the House.
Shelter me under your wing,—
that's all.

* * *

Ты уходишь,
как уходят в небо звезды,
заблудившиеся
дети рассвета,
ты уходишь,
как уходят в небо
на кораблики похожие птицы.

Что вам в небе?
Наша мгла сильнее снега.
Наше солнце
навсегда слабее сердца.
А кораблик
журавля на самом деле –
небольшое
птичье перышко, не больше.

Ты уходишь.
Отпускаю, потому что
опустели
сентябри моими журавлями.
До свиданья.
До бессонных сновидений,
до рассвета,
заблудившегося в мире.

* * *

You're leaving
as stars, the lost
children of dawn,
depart for the sky,
you're leaving
as ship-like birds
depart for the sky.

What's in the sky for you?
Our darkness is stronger than snow,
our sun
forever weaker than the heart.
While the ship of a crane
in fact
is a little
feather of a bird, not more.

You're leaving.
I'm letting you go, for
my cranes
have deserted Septembers.
So long.
Till sleepless dreams,
till the dawn
lost in the world.

* * *

Прощай, Париж!
Летают самолеты,
большое небо в красных параллелях,
дожди, как иностранные солдаты,
идут через Голландию в Берлин.

Прощай, Париж!
Я не уеду боле
туда, где листья падают, как звезды,
где люстры облетают, как деревья,
на улицы квартала Бабилон.

Прости за то, что миллион предчувствий
в моей душе, как в башне Вавилона,
прости мои монгольские молитвы,
монашество мое и гамлетизм.

Прости за то, что не услышал улиц,
моя душа – вся в красных параллелях.
Кто мне сулил исполненное небо?
Такого неба нет и не бывало.

Как убывают люди и минуты!
Атлантов убаюкали моллюски.
Как я умру, не зная, кто из граждан
мне в уши выливал яд белены?

Прощай, прощай и помни обо мне...

* * *

Farewell, Paris!
Jets are flying,
the big sky in red parallels,
like foreign soldiers, rain
marches through Holland to Berlin.

Farewell, Paris!
I will no longer go
where leaves are falling like stars,
where chandeliers shed like trees
onto the streets of the Babylon district.

Forgive me for a million premonitions
in my soul, as in the tower of Babel,
forgive my Mongol prayers,
my monkhood and my Hamletism.

Forgive me for not hearing the streets,
my whole soul in red parallels.
Who promised me the sky of fulfillment?
No sky like that exists or ever did.

People and minutes leave us so quickly!
Mollusks lulled the people of Atlantis.
Could I die without knowing which citizens
poured poisonous henbane in my ear?

Farewell, farewell and remember me…

Письмо

О, вспомни обо мне в своем саду,
где с красными щитами муравьи,
где щедро распустили лепестки,
как лилии, большие воробьи.

О, вспомни обо мне в своей стране,
где птицы улетели в теплый мир
и где со шпиля ангел золотой
все улетал на юг и не сумел.

О, вспомни обо мне в своем саду,
где колокольные звонят плоды,
как погребальные,
                    а пауки
плетут меридианы паутин.

О, вспомни обо мне в своих слезах,
где ночи белые, как кандалы,
и где дворцы в мундирах голубых
тебя ежевечерне стерегут.

Letter

O, remember me in your garden,
where ants have crimson shields,
where large sparrows have spread
their petals lavishly like lilies.

O, remember me in your country,
where birds flew off to a warm world,
where a golden angel on a spire
tried to fly south but failed.

O, remember me in your garden
where fruits are ringing like bells
as at a funeral,
                    and spiders
are spinning meridians of cobwebs.

O, remember me in your tears
where nights are white as shackles
and palaces in pale blue uniforms
watch over you every evening.

Летний Сад Днем

Снег, как павлин в саду – цветной, с хвостом,
с фонтанчиком и женскими глазами.
Рябиною синеет красный холм
Михайловский,– то замок с крышей гильзы!
Деревья-девушки по две в окнах,
душистых лип сосульки слез – годами.
На всех ветвях сидят, как на веках,
толстея, голубицы с голубями.
Их мрачен рот, они в саду как чернь,
лакеи злые, возрастом геронты,
свидетели с виденьями... Но речь
Истории – им выдвигает губы!
Михайловский готический коралл!
Здесь Стивенсон вскричал бы вслух: «Пиастры!»

Мальтийский шар, Лопухиной колер...
А снег идет в саду, простой и пестрый.
Нет статуй. Лишь Иван Крылов, статист,
зверолюбив и в позе ревизора,
а в остальном снег свеж и золотист,
и скоро он стемнеет за решеткой.
Зажжется рядом невских волн узор,
как радуг ряд! Голов орлиных злато
уж оживет! И статуй струнный хор
руками нарисует свод заката,
и ход светил, и как они зажглись,
и пасмурный, вечерний рог горений!
Нет никого... И снег из-за кулис,
и снег идет, не гаснет, дивный гений!

The Summer Garden by Day

Like a peacock, the snow in the garden is colored,
with a tail, a fountain and the eyes of a woman.
The red hill of the Mikhailovsky Palace turns blue
with rowans—it's a castle with a roof of shell-casing!
Tree-maidens, two in each window,
tear-icicles of fragrant lindens, for years.
On all their branches as on the centuries
she and he pigeons sit, fattening.
Their mouths are gloomy, they're like a mob, in the garden,
evil lackeys of geriatric age,
witnesses with visions … But the speech
of History moves their lips!
Mikhailovsky's gothic coral!
Here Stevenson would have shouted: "Piasters."

A Maltese globe, Lopukhina's color…
And snow is falling in the garden, plain, motley.
No statues, only that of Ivan Krilov, a walk-on,
an animal lover in the pose of an inspector,
as for the rest, the snow is fresh and golden,
and soon it will get dark behind the railing.
Nearby, the pattern of the Neva's waves will light up
like a line of rainbows! The gold of eagles' heads
will come to life! With their hands,
a string section of statues will paint the vault of sunset
and the motion of heavenly bodies and how they were lit
and also the gloomy, evening horn of burning!
No one's here … And off-stage snow,
still snowing, divine genius not dying.

* * *

Все прошло. Так тихо на душе:
ни цветка, ни даже ветерка,
нет ни глаз моих, и нет ушей,
сердце – твердым знаком вертикаль.

Потому причастья не прошу,
хлеба-соли. Оттанцован бал.
Этот эпос наш не я пишу.
Не шипит мой пенистый бокал.

Хлебом вскормлен, солнцем осолен
майский мир. И самолетных стай
улетанье с гулом... о, старо!
и ни просьб, ни правды, и – прощай.

Сами судьбы – страшные суды,
мы – две чайки в мареве морей.
Буду буквица и знак звезды
небосклона памяти твоей.

* * *

It's all over, my soul so quiet:
no flower, not even a breeze,
no eyes of mine and no ears,
my heart is a vertical of hardness.

Therefore, I don't ask for communion
or a welcome-mat. The ball is over.
I'm not the one writing this epic of ours.
This frothy glass of mine's not fizzing.

May's world is raised on bread,
salted by the sun. And flocks of planes
flying off with a rumble … oh, nothing new—
no requests, no truth, and—farewell.

Destinies themselves are judgment days;
we're two seagulls in the haze of seas.
I'll be a rune and the sign of a star
in the sky of your memory.

Поэт

1

В какой-то энный, оный, никакой
и винный год, я шел Москвой в заборах,
еще один в России Николай,
мне говорил лир овод Заболоцкий:
уже не склеить форму рифмы в ряд,
нет помощи от нимф и алкоголя,
жим славы протирает жизнь до дыр,
как витязь в шкуре, а под шкурой лег я.
Записывать в язык чужих Тамар,
я труп тюремный, вновь вошедший в моду,
почетный чепчик лавра, премиат,
толст и столетний, буду жить под дубом.
Но только чаще в этот килек клев,
в жизнь – роскошь, груди Грузии, дно денег

2

Восходит в ночь тот сумасшедший волк,
как юность ямба, чистосердный гений.
Тогда беру свои очки у глаз,
их многослойны стекла, чистокровны,
и вижу на земле один залог:
нельзя писать с винтовкой Четьи Новы.
Нельзя светить везде за их жетон
погибшему от пуль при Геродоте,
принц Пастернак сыграл впустую жизнь
Шекспира, поучительное горе.
Рукой Харона – водный калорит! –
переводить за ручку в рощу пары,
нечистой пищи вымытый тарел,
все переводы – это акт неправды.

Poet

1

I walked through the fenced streets of Moscow
some year, that year, no year, a wine year,
one more Nikolai in Russia,
Zabolotsky, the gadfly of the lyres, told me:
there's no way to shape the line with rhyme,
no help from nymphs or alcohol,
the pressure of glory wears holes in a life,
like a Georgian knight, under a hide I lay
to write in a language of alien Tamars.
I am a prison corpse, fashionable again,
a cap crowned with laurels, an award-winner,
stout and centennial; I will be living under an oak.
But often, in this empty-handed life
come luxury, the mountains of Georgia, bottomless money.

2

That crazy wolf rises into the night
like the youth of iamb, like a pure genius.
And then I put on my glasses,
their lenses multi-layered, thoroughbreds,
and see one pledge on earth:
you don't compose a New Testament with a rifle.
You mustn't shine in the glory
of soldiers shot in the time of Herodotus.
Prince Pasternak wasted Shakespeare's
life,—an instructive misfortune.
Charon conveying couples across to the grove
is such a picturesque water-scene
a washed up plate of unclean food!—
all translations are acts of falsehood.

Ворона

И красными молекулами глаз
грустны-грустны, взволнованы за нас

вороны в парке (в нем из белых роз
валетики из влаги и волос).

И вот ворона бросилась. И вот
я все стоял. Она схватила в рот

билетик театральный (как душа
у ног моих он был – дышал, дрожал,

использованный). И остался снег.
Спектакля нет. Вороны нет.

Crow

In the park (where little jacks are
of white roses, moisture and hair)

crows worry about us, the red
molecules of their eyes very sad.

And then a crow rushed. And then
I went on standing. It snapped up in its mouth

a theater ticket (like my soul,
it was at my feet, breathing, trembling,

used up). Only snow remained.
No performance. No crow.

Когда нет луны

Одуванчики надели
белоснежные скафандры,
одуванчики дудели
в золоченые фанфары!

Дождевые вылезали
черви,
        мрачные,
                как шпалы,
одуванчики вонзали
в них свои стальные шпаги!

Паучата – хулиганы
мух в сметанницы макали,
после драки кулаками
маки мудрые махали.

И мигала баррикада
яблок,
        в стадии борьбы
с огурченою бригадой!
Барабанили бобы!

Полем – полем – бездорожьем
(борозды наклонены)
пробираюсь осторожно,
в бледном небе –
                ни луны.
Кем ее
         огонь растерзан?
Кто помирит мир бездонный,
непомерный мир растений,
темнотой загроможденный?

When There Is No Moon

Dandelions put on
snow-white diving suits,
dandelions trumpeted
gilded fanfares!

Earthworms
crawled out,
         gloomy
            as rails,
and into them dandelions
thrust their steel rapiers!

Baby-spiders, hooligans,
dipped flies in sour cream;
wise poppies sawed the air
after fighting.

And the barricade of apples
twinkled when it
           fought with
the brigade of cucumbers!
Beans were beating drums!

I'm making my way with caution,
field to field, along impassable roads
(the furrows tilted)
and in a pale sky—
           there's no moon.
Who tore up
        its flame?
Who will reconcile the bottomless world,
the exorbitant world of plants,
jammed with darkness?

* * *

В дестве,
                где, как говорят, пролог,
спят мои дни досадные.
Детство мое,
                кое прошло
с пятого на десятое,
спады, подъемы зим,
                        а весны –
мизерное количество,
и не колышется клин весны, –
мысленно лишь колышется.

Детство – начало из всех начал:
подлинность в полдни пробуем
лишь поначалу.
                А по ночам –
Подлостью, лестью, пропадом!

Пропадом!
Майский малиновый снег –
пропадом! буднями!
Женщины первой не женский смех –
пропадом!
                тройкой с бубнами!
Детство!
        Напевен и в пору слеп,
правдою – перед правдою
лишь по началу.
                А повзрослев –
прочими препаратами.

* * *

In childhood,
                where, as they say, the prolog starts,
sleep my annoying days.
My childhood
              which was
sporadic:
downs, ups in winters,
and only a few
                of springs—
and the wedge of spring
is not swaying
except in my thought.

Childhood is the beginning of all beginnings:
only at noon do we first try
its authenticity.
                  While at night we try it
by meanness or flattery, and damn-it-ness!

By damn-it-ness!
May's raspberry snow—
by damn-it-ness, by routine!
Your first woman's non-womanish laughter—
by damn-it-ness,
                  by a troika with bells, and damn it!
Childhood!
            Melodic and blind at that time,
by truth—facing the truth,
only at first.
              But having matured—
we try it by other means.

Дом надежд

Дом без гвоздя и без доски.
Брильянт в мильярд карат.
Роняют ночью лепестки
на дом прожектора.

Там алая луна палит,
окорока обожжены,
в бассейнах из хрустальных плит
наложницы обнажены.

Плодово-ягодные! Лавр!
Скотов молочных рык!
Собак благонадежный лай,
резерв зеркальных рыб.

Итак,
над нами Дом Надежд!

Он мудр, как ход комет.
Там нет наветов,
                 нет невежд,
чего там только нет!

Нет одиночек.
                 Не манят
бесславье, власть и лесть.

А также в доме нет меня,
а в общем-то – я есть.

House of Hopes

House without a nail or board.
Million-carat diamond.
Floodlights are dropping
petals on the house, at night.

There a scarlet moon is sizzling,
hams are smoked,
in swimming pools, on crystal tiles
concubines are nude.

Fruit trees and berries! Laurel!
The roar of dairy cattle!
The loyal barking of dogs,
a supply of reflecting fish.

And so,
the House of Hopes is overhead!

It's wise like the course of comets.
No slanderers there,
                              no blockheads,
how many things not there!

No loners.
              Infamy,
power and flattery won't entice.

And there's also no me there,
although, in general, I am.

* * *

> *И все же*
> *наша жизнь – легенда!*

Дурачиться,
               читать сказанья
(страниц пергаментных мерцанье),
героев предавать осанне,
знаменьем осенять мерзавцев.

Макать мечи
               (свирепы слишком!)
в чаны чернильного позора,
учить анафеме мальчишек,
а старцев – грации танцоров.

Дурачиться,
               читать сказанья,
в глаза властителей лобастых
глазеть
лазурными глазами,
от
ненависти
улыбаясь.

Земля моя! Пчела! Дикарка!
Печеным яблоком в духане!
Иду я,
               сказачно вдыхая
и легендарно выдыхая.

* * *

And all the same
our life is a legend!

Fooling around,
                    reading the sagas
(the flicker of parchment pages)
singing hosannas to heroes,
making the sign of the cross over scoundrels.

Dipping swords
                    (they're too ferocious!)
into the vats of inky disgrace,
teaching anathema to boys,
and the grace of dancers to the old.

Fooling around,
                    reading the sagas,
gazing with your azure eyes
into the faces of large
browed rulers,
and smiling
in
hatred.

My earth!—Bee! Savage—
You smell like a baked apple in a diner!
And so I go
                    feeling fabulous inhaling it
and legendary when exhaling.

* * *

Был роскошный друг у меня,

                                 пузатый,

Беззаветный друг –

                       на границе с братом.

Был он то ли пьяница,

                       то ли писатель.

Эти два понятия в Элладе равны.

Был ближайший друг у меня к услугам.

Приглашал к вину

                    и прочим перлам

кулинарии...

               По смутным слухам,

даже англосаксы Орфея пели.

Уж не говоря о греках.

                     Греки –

те рукоплескали Орфею прямо.

То ли их взаправду струны грели,

отклики философов то ли рьяных...

Но моя ладья ураганы грудью

разгребала!

                Струны – развевались!

Праздных призывали к оралу,

                       к оружью,

к празднику хилых призывали.

Заржавели струны моей кифары.

По причинам бурь.

                    По другий отчасти...

Мало кто при встрече не кивает,

мало кто...

Но прежде кивали чаще.

* * *

I had a magnificent friend,
                          a paunchy,
devoted friend—
                          almost a brother.
He was either a drunk
                    or a writer.
In Hellas these two notions are the same.

I had a best friend, always ready to help.
He would invite me for wine
                              and other
culinary gems…
                    According to vague rumors,
even the Anglo-Saxons praised Orpheus,
not to mention Greeks.
                              The Greeks
openly applauded Orpheus.
Maybe strings really warmed them,
or the responses of fervent philosophers…

But my boat cut thorough hurricanes
with its prow!
                    The strings were fluttering!
The idle were called to the plow,
                                   to weapons,
the sick were called to a feast.

The strings of my cithara rusted.
Owing to storms.
                    Owing in part to other reasons…
Almost everyone nods when meeting,
almost everyone…
But they nodded more often once.

Где же ты, роскошный мой,
                         где, пузатый?
Приходи приходовать мои таланты!
Приходи, ближайший мой,
                         побазарим!
Побряцаем рюмками за Элладу!

Над какою выклянченной
                         рюмкой реешь?
У какой лобзаешь пальчики жабы?

Струны ураганов ржавеют на время,
струны грузных рюмок –
                         постоянно ржавы.

Я кифару смажу смолой постоянной.
На века Орфей будет миром узнан.
Ты тогда появишься
                         во всем сиянье,
ты, мой друг,
              в сиянье вина и пуза.

Where are you, my magnificent one,
                              my paunchy one?
Come, keep track of my talents!
Come, my buddy,
                  let's go crazy!
Let's clink our glasses to Hellas!

Which begged wineglass
                              are you hovering over?
Whose toad's fingers are you bussing?

The strings of hurricanes have been rusty for some time,
the strings of heavy wine glasses
                              are rusty always.

I'll lubricate the cithara with lasting rosin.
Orpheus will be known by the world for ages.
Then you will appear
                      in all your radiance,
you, my friend,
                  in the radiance of wine and a paunch.

Кузнечик

Ночь над гаванью стеклянной,
над водой горизонтальной...
Ночь на мачты возлагает
купола созвездий.

Что же ты не спишь, кузнечик?
Металлической ладошкой
по цветам стучишь, по злакам,
по прибрежным якорям.

Ночью мухи спят и маги,
спят стрекозы и оркестры,
палачи и чиполлино,
спят врачи и червяки.

Только ты звенишь, кузнечик,
металлической ладошкой
по бутонам, по колосьям,
по прибрежным якорям.

То ли воздух воздвигаешь?
Маяки переключаешь?
Лечишь ночь над человеком?
Ремонтируешь моря?

Ты не спи, не спи, кузнечик!
Металлической ладошкой
по пыльце стучи, по зернам,
по прибрежным якорям!

Grasshopper

Night hangs over the glassy harbor,
over horizontal water…
Night places cupolas of
constellations on the masts.

> So why don't you sleep, grasshopper?
> You're rapping on the flowers,
> on grain, on coastal anchors
> with your metallic palm.

Flies and wizards sleep at night,
so do dragonflies and orchestras,
hangmen and Pinocchio,
doctors and worms sleep as well.

> Only you are jingling, grasshopper,
> on the buds and ears of rye,
> on the coastal anchors
> with your metallic palm.

Are you erecting air?
switching lighthouses on and off?
Curing the night above a man?
Or remodeling the seas?

> Don't sleep, don't sleep, grasshopper!
> Keep rapping on the flowers,
> on grain, on coastal anchors
> with your metallic palm.

Ты звени, звени, кузнечик!
Это же необходимо,
чтобы хоть один кузнечик
Все-таки
            звенел!

Keep jingling, jingling, you, grasshopper!
for it's essential
at least one grasshopper
still
        keeps jingling!

Сентябрь

Сентябрь!
Ты – вельможа в балтийской сутане.
Корсар!
Ты торгуешь чужими судами.
Твой жемчуг – чужой.
                                    А торговая прибыль?
Твой торг не прибавит
ни бури,
ни рыбы.

А рыбы в берлогах морей обитают.
Они – безобидны.
Они – опадают.
Они – лепестки,
Они приникают
ко дну,
             испещренному плавниками.

Сентябрь!
Твой парус уже уплывает.
На что, уплывая, корсар уповает?
Моря абордажами не обладают.

А брызги, как листья морей, опадают.

Любимая!
Так ли твой парус колеблем,
как август,
                когда,
                           о моря ударяясь,
звезда за звездой окунают колени...

Да будет сентябрь с тобой, удаляясь.

September

September!
You are a dignitary in a Baltic soutane.
A corsair!
You deal in the vessels of others.
Your pearls belong to others.
                              But how about the profits?
Your haggling won't raise
a storm
or a fish.

And fish inhabit the dens of the seas.
They are harmless.
They fall off.
They are petals.
They cling
to the bottom,
                 stippled with fins.

September!
Your sail's drifting off already.
What are the corsair's hopes, when he's drifting off?
Seas don't provide boardings.

And splashes, like sea leaves, are falling.

Darling!
Is your sail as changeable
as August,
            when,
                    hitting the seas,
star after star plunges in, to its knees…

Withdrawing, may September be with you.

Пролог

1

Я семь светильников зажег.
Я семь настольных ламп зажег.
Я семь стеклянных белых ламп
зажег и стол убрал.
Я календарь с него убрал,
когда газетой накрывал,
потом чернильницу умыл,
наполнил целую чернил
и окунул перо.

2

Я окунул неглубоко,
но вынул –
        вспомнил, что забыл
бумагу в ящике стола.
Достал бумажный лист.
Лист – отглянцованный металл,
металл – пергамент.
          Я достал
по контуру и белизне
такой же точно лист.

3

Листы форматны –
          двойники,
вмурованы в них тайники,
как приспособленные лгать,
так искренность слагать.

Prologue

1

I lit seven oil lamps.
I lit seven bedside lamps.
I lit seven glassy white lamps
and cleaned my desk.
I covered it with a newspaper,
as I took the calendar away,
then washed out the inkpot,
filled it to the brim with ink
and dipped in my pen.

2

I only dipped it,
but withdrew—
                        recalling I'd forgotten
the paper in the desk drawer.
I took out a sheet of paper.
A sheet was glossy metal,
the metal—parchment.
                              I got
exactly the same sheet
in contour and whiteness.

3

Sheets formatted
                        are alike,
caches embedded in them,
adapted to lying
or creating sincerely.

Я окунул перо.
                    Пора
слагать!
          Но вспомнил, что февраль,
за стеклами окна февраль.
Вечерний снегопад.

4

Мое окно у фонаря.
Снежинки, будто волоски,
опутали воротники
двух девичьих фигур.

Фигуры женщин февраля
и белозубы, и близки.
Поблескивает скользкий ворс
их грубошерстных шкур.

5

Курили девочки...
                    Они
вечерние, как две свечи.
Их лица – лица-огоньки
у елочных свечей.

Ты, вечер снега!
                    Волшебство!
Ты, ожидание его,
активного, как прототип
мифической любви.

I dipped my pen.
                    It's time
to create!
            But I recalled it was February,
beyond the window-pane was February.
The evening snowfall.

4

My window is by the lamppost.
Snowflakes, like hair,
entangled the collars
of two girlish figures.

The February women's figures
are intimate, with white teeth.
The slippery nap glitters
on their coarse pelts.

5

The girls were smoking…
                        Like two candles,
they belong to the evening.
their faces are the faces of flames
on Christmas-tree candles.

You, the evening of snow!
                        The magic!
You're expectancy of it—
which is active as a prototype
of mythic love.

6

Но ожидаемый – двойник
тех мифов.
              Беспардонно дни
откроют хилое лицо
великих двойников.
Фонарь, ты белка.
                    Ты, обман,
вращай электро-колесо!
Приятельницы – двойники,
окуривайте снег!

7

Я занавеску опустил.
Отполированный листок
настольной лампой осветил.
Я глубже сел за стол.
Я глубже окунул перо,
подался корпусом вперед...
Но вспомнил...осень:
                         о себе
особый эпизод.

8

Стояла осень.
                    О, сентябрь!
Медовый месяц мой, сентябрь!
Тропинка ленточкой свинца
опутывала парк.
Парк увядал...

6

But what you expect is the double
of those myths.
                    Shamelessly, the days
will reveal a sickly face
of the great doubles.
Lamppost, you're a squirrel.
                              You're deceit—
keep spinning the electro-wheel!
Girlfriends are doubles,
keep on shrouding the snow in smoke!

7

I lowered the curtain,
with a table lamp,
shed light on the polished sheet.
I pulled closer to the table.
I plunged my pen in,
moved my body forward…
But I recalled … Fall:
                        a special
episode concerning me.

8

It was Fall.
              Oh, September!
My honeymoon, September!
A path wrapped the park
in a ribbon of lead.
The park was withering…

Среди ветвей,
подобны тысяче гитар,
витали листья.
                        Грохотал
сентябрь:
            – Проклятый век!

9

– Проклятый... –
                        Слово велико!
Велеречиво не по мне.
Благословенных – нет веков.
Проклятых – тоже нет.
Век –
        трогателен он, как плач
влюбленных старцев и старух.
В нем обездолен лишь богач.
Безбеден лишь поэт.

10

Как слезы, абсолютен век!
Прекрасен век!
                        Не понимай,
что абсолютно черный цвет –
иллюзия, искус.
Наглядно – есть он, черный цвет,
есть абсолютный человек,
есть абсолютный негодяй,
есть абсолютный трус!

Leaves hovered
among the branches
like a thousand guitars.
                        September
thundered:
                —Damned century!

9

—Damned...—
                    Powerful word!
The lofty isn't for me.
No blessed centuries exist.
And no accursed ones.
A century as
              touching as the tears
of old men and women in love.
Then only the rich man is unlucky,
only the poet, carefree.

10

The century is perfect as tears!
Wonderful century!
                  Don't take
absolutely black color
for an illusion, a temptation.
There is a color black—it's visible,
there is a perfect man,
there is a perfect scoundrel,
there is a perfect coward!

11

Стоял сентябрь. Сиял сентябрь!
Медовый месяц мой, сентябрь!
Тропа зигзагами свинца
избороздила парк.
Тогда на парк упал туман.
Упал туман,
          и терема
деревьев,
          и огни аллей
невидимы под ним.

12

Тогда туман затвердевал,
как алебастровый раствор,
к лицу приблизишь кисти рук –
и пальцы не видны.
Мы, существа земных сортов,
мы, люди улиц и садов,
как статуи, погружены
в эпический туман.

13

Что было делать? Я стоял
у деревянного ствола.
Я думал в кольцах табака
опять о двойниках.
У каждого есть свой двойник,
у капли, жабы, у луны.
Ты, мне вменяемый двойник,
поближе поблуждай!

11

It was September. September beamed!
My honeymoon, September!
A path furrowed the park
with zigzags of lead.
A fog fell on the park then
Fog fell,
              and invisible
beneath it were
                        huts of trees,
and lights of alleys.

12

The fog hardened then,
like a solution of alabaster;
bring your wrists close
to your face—you won't see fingers.
We, people of the earthly kind,
we, people of streets and gardens,
like statues are plunged
in an epic fog.

13

What could be done? I stood
by a wooden trunk.
Wrapped in smoke rings, I thought
again about the doubles.
There's a double for each of us,
for every droplet, toad, and moon.
You, the double assigned me,
roam a little closer!

[5/]

14

Где ты блуждаешь, мой двойник,
воображенный Бибигон,
вооруженный ноготком,
мой бедный эпигон?
Тебя я наименовал,
ты сброшюрован, издан, жив,
тебе проставлен номинал
истерики и лжи.

15

Ты медлешей меня, модней,
ты – контур, но не кость моя,
акт биографии моей,
мое седьмое «Я» .
Ты есть – актер,

               я есть – статист.
Ты – роковой орган.

                   Я свист.
Ты – маршал стада, стар и сыт,
я – в центре стада –

                     стыд.

16

О, если бы горяч ты

                  был,
как беды голытьбы,
как старый сталевар с лицом
отважно-голубым.
О, если б холоден ты

                  был,

14

Where are you roaming, my double,
my imaginary Bibigon,
armed with a little fingernail,
my poor epigone?
I named you,
you're book-stitched, published, alive,
your face value,
hysteria and lies.

15

You're slower than I, more modish,
you're a contour, not my bone,
an act in my biography,
my seventh "I".
You are the actor,
                    I am the extra.
You're a fatal pipe organ.
                            I'm a whistle.
You're the general of the flock, old and full,
I'm in the center of the flock—
                            what a shame.

16

Oh, were you
                hot,
like disasters of the wretched,
like an old steel worker with a face
bravely blue.
Oh, were you
                cold,

как пот холодный,

            ловкий плач,

но ты не холоден

                и ни

на градус не горяч...

17

Я семь светильников гашу,
за абажуром абажур.
Я выключил семь сот свечей.
Погасло семь светил.
Сегодня в комнате моей
я произвел учет огней.
Я лампочки пересчитал.
Их оказалось семь.

Эпилог

18

Прекрасен сад, когда плоды
созрели сами по себе,
и неба нежные пруды
прекрасны в сентябре.
Мой сад дождями убелен.
Опал мой самый спелый сад,
мой самый первый Аполлон,
мой самый умный Моэм, сад.

like cold sweat,
                    skillful weeping,
but you are neither cold
                              nor
hot at all…

17

I extinguish off seven oil lamps,
one lampshade after another.
I put out seven hundred candles.
Seven luminaries went out.
Today, in my room
I inventoried all my lights.
I counted up my bulbs again.
It turned out there were seven.

Epilogue

18

The orchard is lovely when the fruit
ripens by itself,
and the tender ponds of the sky
and lovely in September.
Rains have aged my orchard.
My heavy orchard shed its fruit,
my very first Apollo,
my cleverest Maugham, my garden.

19

Летайте, листья!
                    До земли
дотрагивайся, лист! Замри!
До замерзанья – до зимы –
еще сто доз зари.
Отгоревал сад-огород,
мой многолапый сад-кентавр,
а листья, листья – хоровод
из бронзовых литавр.

20

Лимит листвы в саду моем?
в студеных дождевых щитах
плывут личинки,
                    их -мильон!..
я прежде не считал.
Любой личинке бил челом...
Но вечно лишь одно число.
Число бессмертно, как вино, –
вещественно оно.

21

Мы сводим счеты, вводим счет.
Лишь цифры соблюдает век.
Одной природе чужд подсчет.
Вот так-то, человек!
Летайте, листья,
                    вы, тела
небес,
        парите и
                за нас...

19

Keep flying, leaves!
                    Leaf,
touch the earth! Freeze!
Before frost comes, before it's winter,
one hundred dawns remain.
My orchard-garden had its share of grief,
my multi-pawed orchard-centaur,
and leaves, leaves do a round dance
of bronze kettledrums.

20

What's the leafage limit in my orchard?
In frozen rainy shields
swim maggots—
                    they're millions!
I hadn't counted them before.
Cap in hand I went to every maggot…
But only one number is eternal.
The number is immortal, like wine,—
it's a substance.

21

We square accounts, we start to count.
A century observes only numbers.
Not everyone cares for calculations.
That's the way it is, man!
Keep flying, leaves,
                    you, bodies
of the heavens,
                    glide for
                              us too…

Ни ритуалов, ни тирад
в саду.
Лишь тишина.

22

Сад – исхудалый хлорофилл...
Зачем сочится седина?
Зачем ты животом не жил,
ты фрукты сочинял?
Плоды полудней дураки
припишут дуракам другим,
твою Песнь Песней – дураку,
тихоне – твой разгул!

23

Фавор тебе готовит век,
посмертной славы фейерверк.
Ты счастлив нынешним:
                        дождем,
дыханьем, сентябрем.
Ни славы нет тебе.
Ни срам
не страшен для твоих корней.
Безмерен сад.
Бессмертен – сам!

No rituals, no tirades
in the orchard.
Only silence.

22

The orchard is thinned chlorophyll…
Why does this graying occur?
Why didn't you follow your stomach,
were you inventing fruit?
Fools will ascribe the fruits
of afternoon labor to other fools,
your Song—as a Song to a fool,
your wild oats to someone mild!

23

The century has a favor in store for you,
fireworks of posthumous glory.
You are happy with today:
                                    with rain
with breathing and September.
You have no glory.
Nor is shame
terrifying to your roots.
The orchard is boundless.
You are immortal!

Отъезд со взморья

Плакать не надо, Вы, – будем как чайки Египта...
Мысли мои несмышленыши – мне вас не додумать.
Надежды мои необитаемые – ни в небе.
Спите, о спите, свирели, как звери, – эхо ваше замерзло.
Женщина, Вы – о любовь детского Дон Жуана!..
Чайки, всё чайки. И море в мокрой сутане.
Солнце соленое ползает, щеки щекочет,
или это кровинки моря мои?
Туман. Знак знакомый луны в океане,
теплая тень сосны на песке последней, в пустыне.
плакать не надо, Вы, – это лицо мое на дне бокала
в той кровинке вина морской, скоморошьей.
Туман – бег белый коня в копытах.
Минет и третий звонок. Пора перекреститься.
(Был скоморох – стал монах. Месть моде.)
Где же четвертый? Не быть. Не услышим.
Плакать не надо, Женщина, Вы, мы оба – только объятья...

Leaving the Seaside

You, you don't need to cry,—we'll be like seagulls from Egypt…
My thoughts are silly—I can't figure them out.
My hopes have no abode—not even in the sky.
Sleep, oh, sleep, pan-pipes, like beasts,—your echo has frozen.
You, woman, are the love of a childish Don Juan!…
Sea gulls, more sea gulls. And the sea in a wet soutane.
The salted sun crawls, tickles the cheeks,
or are these my blood-drops from the sea?
Fog. A familiar sign of the moon in the ocean,
a warm shadow of the last desert pine on the sand.
You, you don't need to cry, —this is my face at the bottom
            of the goblet
in that buffoonery sea, blood-drop of wine.
Fog—the running of a white-hoofed horse.
The third bell will also pass. Time to make the sign of the cross.
(There was a buffoon—became a monk. Revenge on fashion).
Where's the fourth? It isn't to be. We won't hear it.
You, woman, you don't need to cry, we both are only embraces…

Письмо из леса
(вариации)

1

Лист желтый на небе не желтом,
но и не синем.

Иголочки с блеском у елей, а паутина –
как пена.

Воздух воздушен, и где-то там плачут
пчелы.

Вот ветерок, и листья еще
пролетели.

(Помни полет стрекозы и ее кружевце-
крылья!)

Солнце все засевает солнечным
цветом.

Вот я уйду во время луны
в небе.

Запах звериный, но из зверей
лишь я
не вою.

В этом лесу я как с тобой, но ты –
где ты?

Хоть бы оставила боль, но и боль –
былая.

Letters from the Forest
(Variations)

1

A yellow leaf in the sky, neither yellow,
nor blue.

Firs with shining bristles, and a web
like foam.

The air is airy, and somewhere bees
are crying.

There's some breeze and leaves
whisked away.

(Don't forget the flight of the dragonfly and its lace-
wings.)

The sun is sowing everything
with its sunny color.

And so I will leave while the moon
is in the sky.

There's an animal smell, but of the animals
I am the only one
not howling.

In this forest, I'm almost with you, but you—
where are you?

I wish you'd left me pain, but even pain
is gone.

И, запрокидывая лицо свое
к небу,

я говорю: ничего без тебя
мне нету.

2

Зелень цветная, блуд бледнокожих,
лебедь Египта,

мед молока, теплое тело,
нежные ноги,

челка на лбу – инок и конь! –
волосы власти!

Кисти твои не расплести –
так расплескались,

губы твои не целовать, –
замкнуты знаком,

не обнимать хладных колен –
окольцевали,

и на спине спящей твоей
нет мне ладони.

Спи, человек мой голубой,
девочка дочки,

в майской Москве в доме для нас
нет ни паркетки,

And tilting my face back
toward the sky

I'm saying: without you,
I have nothing.

2

Colored greenery, lechery of pallid-faces,
swan of Egypt,

honey of milk, a warm body,
tender feet,

fringes on a brow—monk and horse!
hair of power!

Your wrists cannot be untwined—
they're spilled so wide,

your lips cannot be kissed,—
they're sealed with a sign,

your cold knees cannot be embraced—
banded like birds,

and on your sleeping back,
no place for my palm.

Sleep, my tender one,
a daughter's little girl,

in Moscow in May, we don't own even
a single parquet in the house,

спи, ибо ты ночью – ничья,
даже в объятьях,

снятся тебе глазки машин,
как у китайцев.

Я по лесам, по чудесам
с кепкой скитаюсь,

снова смеюсь и сам про себя
песенку вою:

«Но
он
сел
в
лес
и
пил
лип
сок...»

Стал я так тих и не влюблен,
в буквы играю,

птица ль заплачет – я замолчу –
зверь ли завоет.

Я не приду, я не приснюсь
вовсе ни разу,

но и тебе (клятва!) живой
боль не позволю.

sleep, for you're nobody's at night,
even when embraced,

you dream of cars with narrow
oriental eyes.

I wander through woods and miracles,
wearing my cap,

laugh again and howl
a song to myself:

"But
what's a
star
to
rats,
or a
god
to a
dog?…"

I've become so quiet, and not in love,
I play with letters;

whether a bird cries or a beast howls,
I will keep silent.

I won't return or appear in dreams,
not once,

and I won't (I swear) let you, alive,
hurt me.

[73]

3

Я говорю: ничего без тебя
мне нету.
Я говорю, а ты не услышь
мой шепот,
может, последний в светлом лесу
вопль волчий,
все-таки мало, милая, нам
ласк леса.

Волк запрятался в лист, во тьму, –
знак смерти.
Рыбы ревут немо. В водах –
всхлип, всплески.
Жаворонок задохнулся и не
спас сердце.
Храбрая будь, хороший мой пес,
мой? чей ли?

Заперли в дом, двери на цепь, –
лай, что ли?!
В окна – бинокль, а телефон –
хор Хама.
Все на коленях, – в клятвах, в слезах!
О, овны!
Ты им не верь, ведь все равно
цель – цепью!

Ты так тиха. Шею твою –
в ошейник!
Лишь в полуснах-кошмарах твоих
бред бунта.
Будь же для всех бледной бедой,
бей болью,

3

I'm saying: without you
I have nothing.
I'm saying, though you won't hear
my whisper,
perhaps it's the last scream of a wolf
in the bright woods,
still we can't be happy, sweetheart,
only with the woods' caresses.

The wolf hid in foliage, in darkness—
a sign of death.
Fish roar mutely. In water,
sobs, splashes.
The lark suffocated and his heart,
stopped.
Be brave, my good dog—
mine? whose?

Locked in the house, doors on the chain—
is there barking?
Binoculars at the windows, while the telephone,
a choir of the Boor.
All on their knees, praying and crying!
Oh, Aries!
Don't trust them, all the same—
the aim, in chains!

You are so quiet. Your neck needs
a collar!
They're ravings of revolt
only in your half dormant nightmares.
Be everyone's pale misfortune,
strike with pain,

грешная будь, нелающий мой,
мой майский!

Я ли не мудр: знаю язык:
карк врана,
я ли не храбр: перебегу
ход рака...
Все я солгал. В этом лесу
пусть плохо,
но не узнай, и вспоминать
не надо.

4

Вот я уйду во время луны
в небе.
Наших ночей – нет. И ничто –
время.
Наша любовь – холод и хлеб
страсти
в жизни без жертв – как поцелуй
детства.

Вот муравей – храбрый малыш
мира,
вишенкой он бегает по
веку.
Что для него волк-великан –
демон,
росы в крови, музыка трав
Трон?

В небе ни зги нет. Дерева
тени

be sinful, my unbarking-dog,
born in May.

Am I not wise—I know the language:
the crow is cawing:
Am I not brave: I can cross
the crab's path…
These all are lies. Even if it's bad
in this forest
no need to know
or to remember.

4

And so I will leave while the moon
is in the sky.
Our nights are gone. And time
is nothing.
Our love is the cold and bread
of passion,
living without sacrifices is like
a childhood kiss.

There's the ant—a brave toddler
of the world,
running through the century
like a cherry.
What does he care about a giant wolf-
demon,
dews in blood, the music of Troy's
grass?

The sky is pitch black. Trees have lost
their shadows

порастеряли, или и их –
в тюрьмы?
В нашей тюрьме только зигзиц
числа,
«стой, кто идет?» – выстрел и вопль! -
ты ли?

Только – не ты! Я умолю
утро,
голову глаз выдам своих
Богу,
я для себя сам отыщу
очи...
Не умирай в тюрьмах моих
сердца!

5

Спи, ибо ты ночью – ничья,
даже в объятьях.

Пусть на спине спящей твоей
нет мне ладони.

Но я приснюсь только тебе,
даже отсюда.

Но я проснусь рядом с тобой
завтра и утром.

Небо сейчас лишь для двоих
в знаках заката.

or are they
imprisoned too?
In our prisons there are many
stool-pigeons,
"Stop, who goes there?—a shot and a scream!—
is that you?"

Let it not be you. I'll beseech
the morning,
I will give away the head of my eyes
to God,
I'll find my orbs
myself…
In my prisons of my heart,
don't die!

5

Sleep, for you're nobody's at night,
even when embraced.

Even if on your sleeping back
no place for my palm.

I will still be in your dreams,
even from here.

I will still wake at your side
tomorrow and in the morning.

Now the sky at sunset is
only for two.

Ели в мехах, овцы поют,
красноволосы.

Яблоня лбом в стекла стучит,
но не впускаю.

Хутор мой храбр, в паучьих цепях,
худ он и болен.

Мой, но – не мой. Вся моя жизнь –
чей-то там хутор.

В венах – вино. А голова –
волосы в совах.

Ты так тиха, – вешайся, вой! –
вот я и вою.

Хутора, Боже, хранитель от правд, –
правда – предательств!

Правда – проклятье! С бредом берез
я просыпаюсь.

Возговори, заря для Зверья –
толпища буквиц!

Боже, отдай моленье мое
женщине, ей же!

Тело твое – топленая тьма,
в клиньях колени,

кисти твои втрое мертвы –
пятиконечны,

Spruces in furs, sheep singing
red-haired.

An apple tree bangs its forehead at the window,
but I won't let it in.

My farmstead is brave in spidery chains,
feeble and sick.

Mine, though not mine. All my life
is someone's farmstead.

Wine is in the veins. But the head—
owls in the hair.

You are so quiet,—hang yourself, howl!—
here I howl.

Farmsteads, Oh God, keepers of truths—
truth—the keeper of treacheries!

Truth—a curse! I wake up with
the ravings of birches.

Speak up, dawn for beasts
is a crowd of runes!

Oh God, give my prayer
to the woman, to her!

Your torso— melted darkness,
your knees in cleats,

your wrists three times dead—
pentagonal,

голос столиц твоего языка –
красен и в язвах,

я исцелил мир, но тебе
нет ни знаменья,

жено, отыдь ты от меня, –
не исцеляю!

the voice of the capitals where your language is spoken
is red and ulcerated,

I healed the universe, but there's
not a sign for you,

woman, leave me alone—
I am not healing!

Ночь о тебе

Звезда моя, происхожденьем – Пса,
лакало млеко пастью из бутыли.
И лун в окошке – нуль. Я не писал.
Я пил стакан. И мысли не будили...

о вас... Я не венчал. Не развенчал.
Я вас любил. И разлюбить – что толку?
Не очарован был. И разоча-
рованья – нет. Я выдумал вас. Только.

Творец Тебя, я пью стакан плодов
творенья. Ты – обман. Я – брат обмана.
Долгов взаимных – нет. И нет продол-
женных ни «аллилуия», ни «осанна».

Я не писал. Те в прошлом, – письмена!
Целуй любые лбы. Ходи, как ходишь.
Ты где-то есть. Но где-то без меня,
и где-то – нет тебя. Теперь – как хочешь.

Там на морях в огне вода валов.
(Тушил морями! Где двузначность наша?)
И в водах – человеческих голов
купанье поплавковое... Не надо.

А здесь – упал комар в чернильницу, – полет
из Космоса – в мою простую урну.
Господь с тобой, гость поздний. Поклюем
в чернилах кровь и поклянемся утру.

A Night about You

My star, its origin in Canis,
was lapping milk from a bottle.
No moons in the window. I wasn't writing.
I was drinking. No thoughts stirred me…

about you … I didn't esteem or misesteem you.
I loved you. Stop loving you?—It's senseless.
I was not enchanted. And there is no disen-
chantment—no. I made you up. Period.

Creator of You, I drink the fruits of creation.
You are deception—I am its brother.
No mutual debts. And no con-
tinuation of "hallelujahs" or "hosannas."

I wasn't writing. Those letters are in the past.
Kiss any brow. Walk as you do.
You are someplace. But without me,
and someplace, there's no you. It's up to you now.

There on the seas, the breakers are on fire.
(I extinguished them with seas! Where is our ambiguity?)
And in the waters, human heads
are bobbing … No need.

But here—a gnat fell in the inkpot—a flight
from Space into my modest urn.
God bless you, my late guest. Let's peck
the blood in ink and swear allegiance to the morning.

Дева-рыба

Идешь, как рыба на хвосте. Пол красный.
Нам комната, но в коммунальных скалах.
Шкаф шоколадный. Секретер в монетах.
Оконце – электрическая нефть.
Я брат твой, рыба, Звери моря – оба.
Ты вся на васильковом одеяле.
Объятья животов и бельма бреда
любовного!.. погаснет лампа нам.

Отчаянье ли? Ревность ли по лимфе
александрийской конницей?.. Пастбища
оставим те... Нам – комната, мы – рыбы,
нас – двое. Нам захлебываться тут.
На завтра – труд копыт и крыл Пегаса,
полиция цитат и холод хлеба,
нам – чоканье коленных чашек-здравиц,
шампанские кружочки чешуи!

О, ревом рыбы! Нам хвосты, как в схватке,
и мускулы в узлах, и вопль, и лепет,
нам пальцы – пять и пять на поясницах!
Целую... Отпечатки на сосцах
и пальцев, и ответных поцелуев,
и к жабрам присосавшиеся жабры
лица, и в отворотах междуножий
высасываем языками слизь

зловещую... Узнать – возненавидеть.
Любить – не знать. Мы памятны – все знали:
наитья нет, и нет ни капилляра,
который чьи-то чресла не ласкал,
все волосы всех тел нам не распутать,

[86]

Maiden-Fish

You walk like a fish on its tail. The floor is red.
We have a room, but in communal rocks.
A chocolate cupboard. The desk in coins.
The window is electric oil.
Fish, I'm your brother; we're both sea beasts.
You're stretched out on a blue blanket.
Embracing bellies and blindness of amorous
ravings!… Our lamp will go out.

Is it despair? Or is it jealousy marching through
the lymph like the Alexandrian cavalry? We'll leave
these pastures … We have a room; we are fish,
there are two of us. We will choke here…
Tomorrow—the labor of hooves and Pegasus' wings,
censorship, and coldness of bread,
we will clink kneecaps in toasts,
have champagne ripples of a fish-scale!

Oh, the howl of a fish! We need tails, as in combat,
Muscles in nodes, and a yell and prattle,
we need fingers—five and five on waists!
I kiss … Hickeys on nipples
from both fingers, and responding kisses
and gills stuck to face-gills.
And in between leg flaps,
we're sucking mucus with tongues

sinister … To learn is to hate.
To love is not to know. We recall—knew all:
there's no intuition, not a single capillary
that hasn't caressed somebody's loins;
we can untangle neither all the hair on all the bodies,

бичи бесчестья или зло лобзанья,
а проще – грех не в грех и храм не в храм.

Гул от луны. Проспекты Петербурга.
Уплыть в каналы и легко лакать нам
чужую жизнь, тела чужие, рыба,
блевать под кем попало и на ком.
Так минет труд. Так минет мир. И род мой.
Последний сам, без звука вас, последних
благословляю!.. В келье два девиза:
улыбка и змеиные уста.

nor dishonorable whips nor the evil of a buss;
Or simply—no sin in a sin, no temple in a temple.

A boom from the moon. Petersburg avenues.
Fish, we swim away into canals and it's easier
for us to lap the life of others, the bodies of others,
to vomit, no matter under or on top of whom.
So labor will pass. So the world will pass. So will my kin.
I, the last, soundlessly bless you, last ones!…
There are two mottoes in a monk's cell:
a smile and the lips of the snake.

Жизнь моя

Вот идет моя жизнь, как эстонка, –
озерцо хитрохвостая килька
век овец муравей или вермут
шепот-папоротник в янтаре
эхо солнышка серп в перелесках
капли воздуха крыл воробьиных
вермишелька-березка в болотце
хутор-стеклышко в январе.

Вот идет моя жизнь, моя полька, –
в ореолах волос соловьиных
вол солома осел и Мария
слякоть слов и мазурка-метель
стать-скакун сабля конфедератка
что по ландышам красным копытом
клювы славы орел Краковия
кафедральный крест и мятеж.

Вот идет моя жизнь, как еврейка, –
скрипка-Руфь эра Экклезиаста
урна-мера для звезд златожелтых
за электроколючками культ
йодом Иова храмом хирурга
дециперстная месть Моисея
цифра Зверя за правду праотчью
нас на злато на арфы на кнут!

Так: три девы, три чрева, три рода, –
триединство мое троекровье
что же мне многоженство монголов
глупость флагов глумленье Голгоф
кто я им сам не знающий кто я

My Life

Here comes my life, like an Estonian woman,—
a sly-tailed lake sprat,
age of sheep, an ant or vermouth,
a whisper-fern in amber,
an echo of the sun, sickle in copses,
drops of air from sparrows' wings,
vermicelli-birch in a marsh,
a neat farmstead in January.

Here comes my life, my Polish woman,—
in halos of nightingales' hair,
an ox, straw, a donkey and Mary,
a slush of words and mazurka-snowstorm,
confederate's saber, a robust racehorse,
which smashes lilies with its red hoof,
beaks of glory, an eagle of Krakow,
cathedral cross and rebellion.

Here comes my life, like a Jewish woman,—
violin-Ruth, era of Ecclesiastes,
urn-measure for golden-yellowish stars,
the cult beyond electric thorns,
with Job's iodine, surgeon's temple,
Moses' ten-fingered revenge,
the number of the Beast for a forefather's truth,
gold, harps, the knout for us!

Thus: three maidens, three wombs, three origins,—
my trinity is triple-blooded,
what is Mongolian polygamy to me,
the stupidity of flags, jeering of Calvaries?
who am I to them, I who don't know who I am;

их не их не герой этих гео
дан глагол и я лгу но глаголю
проклиная и их и глагол.

I'm nobody's hero, not a hero of these lands…
a word given, and I lie, but go on wording,
cursing both them and the word.

Уходят солдаты

Лишь спичкой чиркну, и узоры из рта,
кубы, пирамиды, овалы.
Не тот это город, и площадь не та,
и Тибр фиолетов.

В ту полночь мы Цезаря жгли на руках,
о Цезарь! о сцены!
И клялся Антоний стоять на ногах,
и офицеры.

Мы шагом бежали в пустынный огонь,
как ящерицы с гортанью,
сандалии в коже а ноги голы,
из молний когорты.

и до Пиренеев по тысяче рек
мы в Альпы прошли, как в цветочки,
и сколько имен и племен и царей
вели на цепочке.

Триумфы, и лестниц Лондиния стен,
и Нил, и окраины Шара,
на башню всходя и дрожала ступень
от римского шага!

Что это у нас после Мартовских ид?
Лишь склоки Сенату да деньги,
мир замер в мечах, вот когорты идут
по Аппиевой дороге.

На стенах булыжных не тот виноград,
кричали и мулы в конюшнях,

The Soldiers are Leaving

The moment I strike a match designs come from my mouth,
cubes, pyramids and ovals.
It's the wrong city, and the wrong square,
and the Tiber is violet.

That midnight we burned Caesar,
o Caesar, o scenes!
Both Anthony and the officers vowed
to remain firm.

Like lizards, mouths wide,
we trotted into the desert fire,
sandals burn into our skin and legs bare,
cohorts of lightning.

Before the Pyrenees along a thousand rivers
we easily entered the Alps,
leading many names and tribes
and kings on a chain.

The triumphs and stairs off Londinium walls,
and the Nile and the outskirts of the Globe—
when Romans ascended the tower
its steps trembled!

What happened here after the Ides of March?
Only squabbles and moncy for the Senate
world frozen in swords, and cohorts marching
along the Appian Way.

It's the wrong grape on the cobblestone walls,
and even the mules in stables yelled

что Цезарь ошибся, что Октавиан...
А мы не ошиблись.

Тот был Провиденье, Стратег и Фантом,
и пели уже музыканты,
что этот не гений, а финансист,
он – Август, морализатор.

Сбылось, и империя по нумерам.
Но все-таки шли мы в Египет ,
но в мышцах не кровь, а какая-то мгла,
мы шли и погибли.

Пылал Капитолий!.. и пела труба,
и Тибр содрогнулся, и кони! –
О боги, мы сами сожгли на руках
сивиллины книги!

Еще неизвестно, ли Риму конец.
(Вот спички не жгутся, а чиркнул!)
Не тот это голубь, и лошадь – не конь
от Августа до Августишки.

Тибр был – кровеносен в Империи Z.
Не Рим это, тот же, но всё же,
не мрамор кирпич и веревки не цепь,
и Аппий – весь в ветках .

Стальные когорты в оружье ушли,
а было их столько, а сколько?
Хожу, многошагий, они из земли
глядят, как из стёкол.

that Caesar was wrong, that Octavian…
But we were not wrong.

That one was Providence, Strategist and Phantom,
and the musicians were already singing
that this one is no genius, but a financier—
he is Augustus, the moralizer.

It happened: Empire divided by the numbers.
But nevertheless, we marched to Egypt,
with no blood in our muscles, only a haze;
we marched and perished.

The Capitoline was aflame … And a trumpet sang,
both the Tiber shuddered—and horses!
O gods, we ourselves burned
sibylline books!

It's still unknown if Rome is finished.
(I struck matches, but they won't light!)
That's the wrong pigeon, and a mare is no stallion,
starting from Augustus to the despised Augustulus.

The Tiber was the bloodstream in the Empire of Evil.
It's not the same Rome, but still,
brick is not marble, and ropes are not chain,
and all of the Appia is in branches.

Steel cohorts fell to the enemy,
they were so many, but how many?
I walk and walk and, from under the ground,
they gaze as through glass.

II

А кто-то в ту полночь из тех, кто стоял
с зашитыми ртами,
и Доблесть, и Подвиг – оклеветал,
а трубы украли.

Двутысячелетье скатилось, как пот,
народы уже многогубы,
и столько столиц, и никто не поёт, –
украдены трубы!

Как призрак, над крышами стран – электрон
да ядерный рупор.
Не тот это голос! Зачем я, Тритон,
взвывающий в Трубы?

Имперские раковины не гудят,
компьютерный шифр – у Кометы!
Герои и ритмы ушли в никуда,
а новых – их нету.

В Тиргартенах уж задохнутся и львы, –
не гривы, а юбки.
Детей-полнокровок от лоботомий
не будет, Юпитер!

И Мы задохнутся от пуль через год,
и боги уйдут в подземелья.
Над каждым убитым, как нимбы (тогда!)
я каску снимаю.

Я тот, терциарий, скажу на ушко:
не думай про дом, не родитесь,
сними одеяло – вы уж в чешуе
и рудиментарны.

II

And someone, that midnight, among those standing
with mouths sewn up,
slandered Valor and Feat,
and the trumpets were stolen!

The twentieth century rolled off like sweat;
people are multilingual already—
and there are so many capitals, but no one sings;
the trumpets were stolen!

An electron and a nuclear megaphone—
like a ghost—hang over roofs of the country.
That's the wrong voice! Why do I, Triton,
howl on Trumpets?

The imperial shells don't drone,
and the Comet has a computer code!
The heroes and rhythms left for nowhere
and there aren't any new ones.

In the zoos even lions will suffocate—
not manes, but skirts.
There won't be healthy children
because of lobotomies, Jupiter!

And We'll suffocate from bullets in a year,
and gods will leave for caves.
Over each of the killed, like nimbi (then!)
I doff my helmet

I, in the third row, will whisper:
don't think about home, don't be born;
take off your blanket—you are already scaly
and rudimentary.

И ваши пророки, цари и отцы,
горячего солнца мужчины,
как псы, завертятся на «новой» Оси,
как кролики на шампурах.

И больше не будет орлят у орлов,
их яйца в вакцинах.
С березовых лун облетит ореол
без живописных оценок.

И вирус с охватывающим ртом
научит мыслителей Мира,
не хаос, конечно ж, и даже не смерть,
но будут в гармонии срывы.

Смотря из-под каски, как из-под руки,
я вижу классичные трюки:
как вновь поползут из морей пауки
и панцирные тараканы.

Ответь же, мне скажут, про этот сюжет,
Империя – головешки?
А шарику Зем?..
                    Я вам не скажу,
я, вам говоривший.

And your prophets, kings and fathers,
men of the hot sun,
will spin like dogs on a "new" Axis,
like rabbits on spits.

And eagles won't have any eaglets,
their eggs used for vaccines.
Birch moons will shed their halo,
losing picturesque appeal.

Not chaos, of course, and not even death—
but a virus with an encircling mouth
will teach the World's thinkers—
though there will be breakdowns in this harmony.

Looking from under a helmet as from under a hand,
I see classical tricks:
spiders and carapaced cockroaches
will crawl from the seas again.

You there, I'll be told, answer us:
is the Empire embers?
how about the Eart…
                        I won't tell you,
I, who have been talking to you.

По февралю

Давно, что, может быть, чуть слышно,
среди озёр, где лунный тон,
скажи, когда-нибудь счастливой,
не отвечаю, и не то.

И жили мы, уже чужие,
но всё же двое, а теперь,
и маски гипсовой, тяжелой
твоей вражды я не терпел.

Но в этот век мечтать о ветке
из соловьев, – в который раз,
как два сокамерника в клетке,
и кто кому погасит глаз.

А может быть, еще возможно,
я выну карту короля,
а может быть, еще возьмёмся,
я украду тебе коня.

И мы умчимся в Дом Надежды,
и Смерть повесим на суку,
и этот саван не наденут,
в ногах лампаду не зажгут.

А может быть, конь бег убыстрит,
иголкой спрячешься в саду,
и не найдёт тебя Убийца,
я выйду, что-нибудь солгу.

А может быть, обиняками
я Коменданту стану друг,

In February

By lakes the color of the moon,
in the distant past which lingers still—
tell me, were you ever happy;
no answer; wrong question.

And so we lived, already strangers,
but still the two of us, though now
your animosity and heavy
plaster mask were hard to bear.

These days a branch of nightingales
even in dreams is a rare sight.
We're often two cellmates in a cage.
And who will put out whose light?

And maybe, there's a chance as yet
for me to draw the king, a coup,
and maybe, we can still take action,
I'll make off with a horse for you

We'll gallop to the House of Hope,
and hang Death from the limb of a tree,
and they won't dress you in a shroud
and light a candle at your feet.

Or maybe the horse will quicken its pace,
you'll hide yourself like a needle in
the garden, the Assassin won't find you,
while I will face and lie to him.

Or maybe somehow I'll attain
the friendship of the Commandant,

и твою карту обменяю,
и твою пулю – мне дадут.

Моих литот, моих гипербол
остался, может быть, стакан,
уж на чешуях от гитары
ещё поет тебе цыган.

О эти черные чешуи,
как перья коршуна зари,
в твоей стране живут чужие
и лгут свои календари.

Давно уехали кибитки,
и листопад лежит спиной,
краплёных нет, все карты биты,
и всё же ты побудь со мной.

За эти звуки горловые,
моя цыганская звезда,
кричали руки голубые,
что не сойдутся никогда.

Я только руки отгибаю
от умирающей груди,
но эти руки голубые
не отогнуть, не уходи.

Я чужеземец, и по крови
никто, помощник, не придёт,
я руки пальцами покрою,
и этот холод отойдёт.

У нас все годы високосны,
и нет ни завтра, ни потом,

and I will exchange your card,
and, in your stead, will get the bullet.

Of my litotes and hyperboles
perhaps there remains not much more
while a gypsy goes on singing to you
on the fish-scales of his guitar.

O these ebony fish-scales
are like a hawk's plumes at sunrise;
strangers are living in your country
and your own calendars tell lies.

Long ago the wagons left,
and autumn leaves lay on their backs.
There're no marked cards, the game is up;
still, stay with me awhile.

In answer to these guttural sounds—
gypsy star of mine—
azure hands were crying out
that they would never meet again.

I only try to unbend the arms
from the breast of someone fading,
but those azure arms refuse
to be unbent—don't go away.

I'm a stranger—by my blood,
a no-one, no helper will show up.
I'll cover your hands with my fingers
and this coldness will depart.

Every year's a leap year here—
no tomorrow, no afterward,

а эти стены ввысоченны,
и не взорвать казенный дом.

Я эти стены обиваю
безумным лбом, и у груди
я эти руки обливаю,
и обовью, – не уходи.

Не уходи, она посмеет
тебя забрать по февралю,
и плач постыдный и посмертный
тебе, живой, я говорю.

but these walls are very high
and the prison won't blow up.

I'm beating on these very walls
with my mad brow, and shed tears on
the hands at your breast, and I'll
entwine them there—don't go away.

Don't go away, Death will try
to take you off in February—
my shameful and posthumous weeping,
to a still breathing you, I say.

* * *

Я не хочу на карту звездной ночи,
закопанный, хоть это ни к чему,
по мне идут империи и ноги,
я слышу орудийные шумы.

Я вижу воздух, молнии паденье,
я вижу спички вспыхнутых комет,
я мог бы выйти, но куда пойду я,
я мог бы петь, но в голосе комок.

Зачем мне тазобедренные кости,
и череп, и цветы посмертной лжи,
вот две ноги лежат, как водостоки,
при жизни я не помню, чтоб лежал.

А если и, то и не на Сиренах,
мне девять Муз не пачкали чело,
и сколько, карий, глаз я трогал синих,
земные ню, – несметно их число.

Я не таился, как фонарь секретный,
я шел по Солнцу, освещая грязь,
а тут чужие шепчутся скелеты,
что на плите моей златая вязь.

Ваш Шар замёрзнет, выключен, потухнет,
меня завидя в прорезях Пяти,
и Бог уйдёт в магнитные потоки,
скользя по пряжкам Млечного пути.

Как нуль, посудомойщик Мирозданья,
в светящейся нейтринной пелене,

* * *

I don't want to be on the map of a starry night,
buried; no need for that;
empires and feet are marching over me,
I hear the noise of guns.

I see the air, the falling lightning,
I see the matches of flaring comets,
I could have surfaced, but where would I go,
I could have sung, but there's a lump in my throat.

What do I need hipbones for,
or a skull, or flowers of a posthumous lie;
here, like drainpipes, two legs are lying,
I don't remember lying that way alive.

But even if I did, it wasn't on the Sirens;
the nine Muses didn't soil my brow;
I touched so many hazel and blue eyes,
the earthly nudes are countless.

I didn't hide like a secret streetlamp;
I walked on the Sun, lighting the dirt,
but here the skeletons of strangers whisper
that on my tombstone there's a golden script.

Your Globe will freeze, turned off, and die
on seeing me in the slits of the Five,
and God will go to magnetic streams,
sliding on buckles of the Milky Way.

In a luminous neutrino mist,
holding down a pinky-finger

уйдёт, отставив с пальчиком мизинчик
с навинченными кольцами планет.

и убежит, как бешеный, за ширмы
закройщик глин и прочих униформ,
и каждый шаг, увешанный Шарами,
звонит, как алкоголем, у него!

Я говорил, сожгите это тело,
снимите имя с книг и что о них,
я буду жить, как пепельное эхо
в саду династий автор-аноним,

где, может быть, не всё и голубое,
но не склоняют ветви дрожи ив,
где нет ни чугуна над головою,
ни пальцев, указательных, как Вий.

Здесь льётся кровь людей, как водопады,
и серый снег всеобщих метастаз,
я не хочу ни в Ямбы, ни в Адепты,
где, что ни встречный, смертник и мутант.

Я жил уже, у индов пересмешник,
и повторим, как метеор на Мир,
я жду агон, чтоб выйти перед смертью
туда, где нет ни Я, и ни Меня.

with screwed on rings of planets,
the dishwasher of the Universe will leave like a nobody.

And will flee like crazy behind the screens,
a tailor of clays and other uniforms,
and his every step, hung with Globes,
resounds like alcohol!

I was saying: burn this body,
remove his name from books and reference to them,
I will live like an ashen echo,
an anonymous author in the garden of dynasties,

where, perhaps, not everything is blue,
but trembling willows don't bend their branches,
where there's no cast-iron over your head
nor forefingers like Vee's.

Here, the blood of people flows like waterfalls,
and the snow of universal metastasis is gray;
I don't want to be in Iambs or among Adepts,
where you only meet mutants or death row inmates.

I previously lived, a mockingbird with the Inds,
will come again, as a meteor to the Earth;
I await my agony so that I can meet death
and go, where neither I nor Me exist.

* * *

Эрос не рос.
Ведь дева была без подушки. В ванне, одна.
Отключили краны и душ.
Я ее поливал кипятком. Шипела.
Но эрос не рос.
Маленький мой огонек не поднимался столбом.
Я ведро вскипятил. Сел, как соловей.
Эрос не рос.
Члены мои леденели, как дети.
Чресла ее пошли пузырями, ожоги.
Я дал ей супа.
Суп не помог (в миске москитной).
Ожоги мешали оргазму так чрезвычайно,
как от изжоги и как ежи.
– Что бендем делать? -спросил я.
– «Скорая помощь»!
Восемь врачей нас растирали.
Но эрос не рос.
И только когда полилась
из крана серая струйка –
эрос раздался!
Подушка пришла.
И на подушке сидя и плача от первого раза,
душ зашумел!
Эрос раскрылся.

* * *

Eros wouldn't rouse.
Because the maiden had no cushion—in the bath, alone.
Taps and shower were off.
I watered her with boiling water. She hissed.
But eros wouldn't rouse.
My little flame wouldn't rise like a column.
I boiled a bucketful. Sat down like a nightingale.
Eros wouldn't rouse.
My members froze like children.
Her loins began bubbling—burns.
I gave her some soup;
soup (in a mosquito tureen) didn't help.
The burns blocked an orgasm completely
the way heartburn or hedgehogs do.
What'll we do?—I asked.
—"An ambulance!"
Eight physicians rubbed us.
But eros wouldn't rouse.
But the moment a gray stream
from the tap began flowing
eros grew larger!
And the maiden sat
on the cushion, and wept
after the first relief,
the shower began humming!
Eros had opened.

День надежд

День мой деньской одеяний!
Надел широкую шпагу.
Широкую рожу надел на узкие зубы.
Надел на демона девушку без перчаток.
Надел на глазницы (ей) бюстгальтер – лучше очков!
Штаны не надел, девушка ведь надета!
Что бы еще надеть? –Шляпу. Надел.
Одет недостаточно. К шубе шагнул.
Девушка не сходит, сидит на демоне,

как на стременах.

Ну что ж, ну что ж.
Надену еще шаль шерстяную
себе на спину, ей на грудь.
Не видит, визжит:
– Не надевай, я ж обнаженка!
Сидели в то утро мы
с девушкой, так надетой,
что и не вывинтишь.
И так – часов пять.
Потом мы оба надели делирий
и развинтились.
Лежали, дрожа!
Ели с ноги простоквашу.
Слава богу, хоть к ночи
мне удалось одеться во что-то из меха.
Это «из меха» – сестра ея. Все же надежда
на теплые отношения.
А третья сестра под нами легла, как диван.
Так, троеборцы, они одели меня, без меня.
Ведь я их взял не умом.
А демонизм? Обаянье? Шляпа до плеч?

Day of Hopes

This day of mine, full of dressing!
Put on a broad rapier.
Put a wide mug on narrow teeth.
Put a girl without gloves on the demon.
Put a bra on eyes (hers)—better than glasses!
Didn't put on pants—the girl had been put on already!
What else to put on? A hat. Put it on.
Not enough clothes yet. Approached the fur coat.
The girl won't get off; sits on the demon

                                as if in stirrups.

Oh well, oh well.
I'll also put a wool shawl
on my back, on her breast.
She doesn't see, shrieks:
Don't put it on, I'm a nudist!
That morning I was sitting
with the girl put on in such a way
you couldn't unscrew her.
Like that about five hours.
Then we both put on delirium
and came unscrewed.
We lay shivering!
Ate yogurt from a leg.
Thank God, by night
I managed to put on something furry.
This "something furry" was a sister of hers. Hence, a hope
for warm relations.
And a third sister lay beneath us like a sofa.
Thus, these tri-athletes dressed me, without my help.
It wasn't by mind that I conquered them.
By demonism? Charisma? A hat to the shoulders?

Одна как стена, вторая как циркуль,
третья – диван волосяной.
И я. Под луной многострунной
мы плохонько пели
в комнатке-колбе.
Помню – не помню я тот еще фестиваль!

The first sister's flat as a wall, the second, like dividers,
the third—a hairy sofa.
And me. Under a multi-stringed moon
we sang awfully
in a retort-like room.
That was some kind of festival!—remembered or not.

Август

Улитка с корзинкой,
лягушки стоят на камнях, как сфинксы,
и ветр в осинах!

Мышь,
с лапкой.

Дрозды, целой стаей, у ягод.

Звезды всё ближе.

Сверчок!
кто-то уйдет.

August

A snail with a basket,
frogs standing on stones like sphinxes,
and wind in the aspens!

A mouse
with a paw.

An entire flock of thrushes around the berries.

Stars closer and closer.

A cricket!
someone will leave.

Эпилог

1

Почему в этом доме
деревянные башни,
голубиные яйца?
и сверчки будто вспышки
выстрелов у дверей?

2

Кисти ломаются, руки кружат по лицу,
задевая уши, смотрю туч на смену,
одно на другое, и капли льнут к лицу
из Верховной слизи.
И женщины в тучах капли льют
и приникают к лицу,
но смена женщин и смена туч –
одни и те же дожди.

3

Не называй. Сказанное громко отодвигает тебя в небытие.
Кислые кости не ешь, а отстрани.
Голубиные яйца сожми указательным пальцем и большим,
брызнет сок на твою хиромантию и осязай.

4

О как ранят старые предметы,
керамические их монеты,
свечка Фарадея, клавесин,
поколенья клавиш из кости
слоновой...
И снежинка Кеплера.

Epilogue

1

Why does this house
have wooden towers,
pigeon eggs?
and crickets like volleys
of shots at the doors?

2

Wrists break, hands swirl around the face,
touching ears; I look at the change of clouds,
one on another and drops from Heavenly mucus
cling to the face.
And women in the clouds shed drops
which cling to the face,
but the change of women and change of clouds
are one and the same rains.

3

Don't name. A loudly spoken word moves you into non-existence.
Don't eat sour bones: put them aside.
Squeeze pigeon eggs between your index finger and thumb,
the juice will spurt on your palm reading; feel it.

4

O, how old things hurt,
their ceramic coins,
Faraday's candle, a clavichord,
generations of ivory
keys …
And Kepler's snowflake.

5

Как стерегут костры зеленые огни…
. . . .
Ну вот. Двери закрываются. Выход и вход
забиты гвоздями в шляпках на тонком каблуке,
и вылезаю – крысы рисуют пол,
древоточцы в боксерских перчатках шлют салют из щелей,
пауки забрасывают сетями углы и столы.
Не иллюзорно как-то.

6

О сколько лет прошло с тех зим
и съедено камней.
русалок бюст и женщин низ –
тела давно минувших дней…
Мне скучно, негус!

7

И день и ночь ходить как дом
с ветрами туч – и ходуном,
с одним окном, с одним огнём
и деревянным дном,
и сыплются в тартарары
лишь черепицы с головы!

8

Вот что:
когда онемеет нейронная голова,
это ничего,
сделай сам дубликат из фарфора и разрисуй,
а ту вынь, а эту вставь,

5

How bonfires keep watch over green flames…
……
And so. The doors are closing. Exit and entrance
are hammered with nails, heads on a stiletto heel,
and I crawl out—rats paint the floor,
woodborers in boxing gloves send a salute from cracks,
spiders fling their nets over corners and tables.
Far from an illusion.

6

O how many years have passed since those winters
and how many stones consumed.
the busts of mermaids and the bottoms of women
are bodies from days long gone…
I'm bored, Negus!

7

Both day and night, to sway
like a house full of cloud winds,
with one window, one fire
and a wooden base,
and only tiles from the head
are pouring to hell!

8

Here's what:
when a neuron head numbs
it's okay;
make a duplicate of porcelain and color it,
then take out the old, insert the new

и ты увидишь много нового, к примеру – лохань,
выдолбленную из осины, где моется ню,
пальчиками отшлифовывая свой организм.
О новость! Да сколько этих ню ни мой,
а мыл! Новости нет, тысяча – как одна и та ж.
Лучше помой сигарету...
Жгу теин.

9

Бегу и бегу, включив все четыре колеса,
как идеома бега: не к а от,
обходя попеременно то жизнь, то смерть,
и в конце концов – конца нет.
В этой книге даже имен – ни одного,
даже тоски, столь излюбленный метод туманов – не черчу.
гирлянды шифровок и санкюлота красный колпак,
штаны Пифагора – штаны санкюлота – равны.
А кто они? – циркуль у ног у круга, куда ни беги,
негасимая лампа с гальваникой перпетуум мобиле
                                        в энность нулей,
фельетон, запрятанный в маску, будто б мист,
действуя дрелью, как языком телег
в приступе белой горячки выпив уксус вместо вина
в ванне, – кричи Платону с Алкивиадом:
– Закон! Закон!
...Ишь ты, какой какао-Сократ (на вид!)

and you will see much new, for example, a washtub,
hollowed from an aspen, where a nude washes,
polishing her body with fingers.
Big news! No matter how much you wash those nudes,
and I did, there's no news. A thousand is the same as one.
Better wash a cigarette…
I'm drinking scorching tea.

9

I run and run, engaging all four wheels,
like the idea of a race—not towards but from,
evading alternatively life and death,
and, in the end, there is no end.
There are no names in this book, not a single one,
I don't draw even yearning, that favorite trait of fogs.
not even garlands of codes and the sansculotte's red cap,
the trousers of Pythagoras and a sansculotte's are equal.
But who are they?—a divider at the feet of a circle,
                                        wherever you run,
an eternal lamp with the galvanism of perpetual motion
                                        to some zeros,
a feuilleton, hidden in a mask, like a mist;
using a drill like the tongue of carts
in a fit of delirium tremens, drinking vinegar
instead of wine in the bath ,—shout to Plato and Alcibiades:
Law! Law!
…Hey you, you excitingly brisk Socrates (in appearance)!

10

Ну налетай на телегу , я двух жен любил и убил (в стогу!)
и устал я, соломенный, в белых кудрях,
а для чего же пишет писец? –
у веских признаний аргументов – нет.
сколько любви вокруг, ими полны моря
и подземелья, и норы и шум шелковиц,
лишь на Земле две ноги
лежат, вечнозеленые, – между двух других.

11

Ни души. Я ломаю карандаши,
чтоб не записывать. Магма под садом кипит.
Вишни взошли – как дубы! в желудях!
Сливы – как пломбы!
Чашку беру за ручку и зачерпнул из пруда лягушачьей
                                                                              икры, –
мертвая! Цапле не будет урожая лягух.
А я играю на клавишах, слева басовый, справа
                                                                скрипичный
                                                                      ключ,
оба они от двери. (Двери закрываются.)

12

На пружинах перегибы,
открывается кровать,
спи, дитя моё, погибель,
метастазное тавро!
· · · · · · · · · · · · · · · ·
Ах, лунный всадник за мной скакал!

10

Well, attack the cart; I loved and killed two wives (in a haystack!)
and I'm tired, a grass-widower, with blond curly hair,
then what is a scribe writing for?—
valid confessions have no arguments.
there's so much love around, the seas are filled with it,
and caves, and burrows and noise of mulberry trees;
there are two legs only on Earth
lying, evergreen, between two others.

11

Not a soul. I break pencils,
in order not to write. Magma boils under the orchard.
Cherries fruited! like oaks with acorns!
Plums like fillings!
I take a cup by the handle and scoop some frog-caviar
            from the pond—
it's dead! The heron won't be harvesting frogs.
And I'm playing on the keys, bass clef to the left, treble
            to the right;
both for the door. (The doors are closing.)

12

Springs are bent,
the bed is opening,
sleep, my child, my disaster,
metastatic brand!
. . . .
Ah, the lunar rider galloped behind me!

13

О спите усталые Силы,
я вам не подвластен,
и это я виноват за тучи чаек,
что били саблями Эру Рыб.
Рыбы уйдут в одиночку, в заплыв, как будто вдвоем уходят,
и мой боевой жест неоспорим,
я ничего, а диаспоры устали.
В теле гвоздей есть зазубрины. –
Мои заветы новым богам,
это и есть конец
белого безмолвия, тренинг смерти? –
как ноздри кабана со множеством колец!

14

О четырех стенах плакучая береза,
декабрьских листков еще полным-полно,
свисают надо мной ея стеклянны бусы.
со свистом на одном быть может лепестке.

15

Миндаль и медь, и чьи сибиллы
тебя (прошепчено!) – вернёт?
иду ко рту за сигаретой,
и чернокнижный том – Вермонт.
Поход детей к Иерусалиму,
и красный плащ Тибетских лам?
надеты челки на ресницы,
сквозь сетку – кто и кем любим?
Я сжег тебя и пепел жизни
развеял ногтем, где камней. ..
но и меня унес из жести, –

13

O, sleep, tired Forces,
you have no power over me,
and it's I who is guilty of seagull clouds
that hit with sabers The Age of Pices.
The fish will go, swimming solo, as if two by two,
and my militant gesture is irrefutable,
I'm okay, but the diasporas are tired.
There are notches in nails' bodies.—
Are my behests to new gods—
are those then the end
of white silence, training for death?
they're like a hog's nostrils with multiple rings!

14

Surrounded by four walls, a weeping birch
still full of December leaves,
trails with a whistle over me its glossy beads,
probably hanging on a single petal.

15

Almond and copper, and whose sibyls?—
will bring you (whispered) back?
I reach for the cigarette in my mouth,
and a black leather volume of Vermont.
Will a children's march to Jerusalem,
and a Tibetan lama's red coat do it?
fringes are put on lashes,
through a veil—who is loved by whom?
I burnt you and scattered the ashes of life
with a fingernail where stones…
but I also kicked the bucket,—

такой вот и крылообмен?
Просвечен пленкой азимута,
и шепчет Голос голубой,
что это двух телекинеза
воспеты ветром, не рукой!

P. S.

Это третья сюита из Книги конца,
пятнистый по́лоз, черный уж и бичевидная змея,
певчий ястреб живущий на юге Африки, и он поёт так:
кэк-кэк-кэк или же кик-кик-кик,
довольно хорошая песенка – для заик...
четвертой не будет...

that's how it goes.
Transluminated by the film of the azimuth,
a pale blue Voice whispers
that these two telekinesis
are glorified by wind, not by hands!

P.S.

It is the third suite from the Book of the End,
a dappled sled-runner, a black grass snake and a twine-like serpent,
a singing hawk living in the south of Africa, and it chants so:
kitterers-kitterers-kitterers or kutterers-kutterers-kutterers,
a fairly good ditty for stutterers…
there won't be a fourth…

JUNE 2000—APRIL 2001

[131]

NOTES

Boyan's Gusli:

Here *Boyan* is simply the name of a person, but with the suggestion that it is someone from the distant past. The Boyan were a Neolithic people (4,000 B.C.) who lived in the area of Rumania (where there is a Lake Boyan), Bulgaria, and Moldavia.

Gusli: a Russian, zither-like stringed instrument.

Mstislav, Prince Rededya: Rededya was a prince of the Adygis (also known as the Kasogs in Russian chronicles), beaten in 1022 in single combat by the Tmutarakansky Prince Mstislav.

Kalika

Kalika: a wandering minstrel, usually blind. Such minstrels appear in Russian folk epics.

Uncle-Ivans: Дядьки-ваньки [Dyad'ki-van'ki] [Uncle-Ivans] is probably based on Ванька-встанька [Van'ka-vstan'ka], a Russian doll constructed so that it can't stand upright.

Appeal

Cainists: a sect in tsarist Russia that would gather at night to repent their treacheries. They lit icon lamps to check that everyone repented sincerely.

Farewell, Paris

Babylon: a street in Paris on which the poet Louis Aragon and his wife Elsa Triolet lived. The Soviet embassy was also located there.

The Summer Garden by Day

The Summer Garden in St. Petersburg has more than 150 statues, one of which is a bronze figure of Ivan Krylov (1769-1844), best known for his fables. The garden is enclosed by a grill, topped with various imperial decorations—the two-headed Romanov eagle among them. It is bordered on one side by the Neva, the chief river of St. Petersburg, and on the other by the Mikhailovsky Garden, which ends at the rear of the Mikhailovsky Palace.

Maltese globe: the Maltese Order had a crystal globe symbolizing the cosmos.

Lopukhina: a mistress of Tsar Pavel. She wore gloves of a coral shade. Pavel ordered the palace painted that shade.

Poet

Nikolai Zabolotsky: (1903-58) was one of a group of poets in Leningrad associated with the OBERIU literary movement. Arrested in the late 1930s, he survived the gulag and went on to translate the old Slavic epic "Lay of Igor's Campaign" into modern Russian.

Queen Tamar: (1184-1213) ruled during the period of Georgia's greatest power and prestige. The supreme literary achievement of this age was Shota Rustaveli's epic poem, "The Knight in the Panther's Skin."

The poet and novelist Boris Pasternak (1890-1960) is also famous as a translator of Shakespeare. He translated *Hamlet*, and a well-known poem of his own (included in *Dr. Zhivago*) is written in Hamlet's voice.

Prologue

Bibigon: *The Adventures of Bibigon* is a children's story in prose and verse by Kornei Chukovsky.

My Life

geo: land or lands.

The Soldiers Are Leaving

Londinium: Latin for London.

part 2

"in the third row": In the Roman army different roles were assigned to men located at different points in the line. If the first two rows fell into disarray, veterans in the third row would advance with a battle cry in order to cheer the young soldiers and frighten the enemy.

I don't want to be on your map

Vee: a mythological Slavic spirit of death having heavily lidded, enormous eyes that kill with a single look.

slits of the Five: the ancient Egyptians and Greeks had a Solar System consisting of five planets.

Inds': Инды [Indy], Sosnora's neologism combining "Hindus" with the river "Indus."

Epilogue

"the doors are closing": In the metros of St. Petersburg and Moscow, just before a train departs, the loudspeakers inside the car announce: "Careful, the doors are closing."

Negus: Sosnora here uses the Ethiopian imperial title of Negus as the name of an Egyptian god.

"excitingly brisk Socrates": The Russian какой какао-Сократ [kakoj kakao-Sokrat] [some cocoa-Socrates] is intended to intensify the metaphor, according to Sosnora, and is based on the nature of "alliteration and cocoa, both of which are exciting."

PS:

"there won't be a fourth.": Russians have traditionally called Moscow "The Third Rome" (after Rome itself and Constantinople). A sixteenth-century monk predicted as he conferred the title of "Caesar" (tsar) on Vasily III, "a fourth there will not be."

Other titles from the series

IN THE GRIP OF STRANGE THOUGHTS

A series of books featuring poets introduced in the bilingual anthology In the Grip of Strange Thoughts: Russian Poetry in a New Era, *which presents poetry at the critical turning point away from Soviet life to a reclamation and renewal of Russian culture and individual voices.*

Salute to Singing
Gennady Aygi
Translated by Peter France

These variations on folkloric themes are born out of the Chuvash and Turkic motifs that Aygi grew up with, and which Aygi and France have collected in their work on Chuvash poetry. A Turkic language, Chuvash is spoken by about a million and a half people in and around Chuvashia—formerly an autonomous republic of the USSR—located 500 miles east of Moscow. Now in his 60s, Aygi continues to be celebrated as the Chuvash national poet, and as a major poet of the Russian language.

"Peter France's scrupulous versions are faithful not simply to the often ambiguous sense of the originals, but also to the typographical minutiae … which spell out the exclamations, questionings, pauses, vulnerabilities and praises of this most remarkable poet."
    —TIMES LITERARY SUPPLEMENT

Poetry / 96 pages
Paper (0-939010-69-0) $12.95

The Score of the Game

Tatiana Shcherbina

Translated by J Kates

Shcherbina emerged in the early 1980s as a spokesperson for the new, independent Moscow culture. Her work was first published in the official press of the Soviet Union in 1986, and five volumes of her poetry were published in samizdat prior to 1990. Her poetry is now widely published in both established and experimental journals at home and abroad, and has been translated into Dutch, German, French, and English. Shcherbina's poetry blends the personal with the political, and the source for her material is pulled from classical literature, as well as French and German cultural influences.

Poetry / 136 pages
Paper (0-939010-70-4) $12.95

A Kindred Orphanhood

Sergey Gandlevsky

Translated by Philip Metres

An integral member of the Seventies Generation, Gandlevsky was one of the underground Russian poets who wrote only for themselves and their circle of friends during the Brezhnev era. Despite their relative cultural obscurity—or perhaps, precisely because of their situation as internal émigrés—the Seventies Generation forged new directions in Russian poetry, unfettered by the pressures that burdened Russian writers both before and during the Soviet period.

"Out of the Rubik's Cube of Russia rise the complex strains of Sergey Gandlevsky ... superb translations that uncannily make the Russian ours." —ANDREI CODRESCU

Poetry / 136 pages
Paper (0-939010-75-5) $12.95